PENGUIN B(

Cake

BIBLE

Cake

BIBLE

Introduction

Cake baking is a wonderfully rewarding cooking skill that many of us have picked up from an early age. Many of us remember helping Mum or Grandma in the kitchen, stirring the cake batter and being lucky enough to lick the spoon or bowl at the end of the mixing!

There is nothing more delightful than coming home to the heady aroma of a freshly baked cake. Home-made cakes are great for afternoon teas, fund-raising stalls, dinner parties and special celebrations, and make lovely birthday or Christmas gifts. They don't necessarily have to be elaborate — a simple dusting of icing sugar on top is often all they need to make them special.

All the recipes in this book were designed to be quick and easy to prepare, with simple methods and no need for fancy tins or equipment. The recipes include traditional family favourites that will remind you of your childhood, as well as some fresh new ideas to impress your friends and family and get your tastebuds tingling.

Hints for baking cakes

- Whichever cake you are making, preparation is important. Use good quality ingredients, pay attention to measurements and check the heat of your oven.

- Make sure you have a suitable cake tin and grease, line or dust it with flour before preparing the cake mixture. If this is not done properly the cooked cake will stick to the tin and break up when you try to turn it out.

- Preheat the oven to the required temperature. If the oven is not hot enough the cake will not rise well and will be heavy. If the oven is too hot the outside of the cake will burn before the inside is cooked. The mixture should be baked immediately to give good results.

- Measure out all the ingredients first, before starting to make the cake batter.

- Eggs, butter and oil are best used at room temperature.

- The egg size used in most recipes is medium (approximately 60 g); where large size is specified, use 65 g eggs.

- When creaming butter and sugar use a wooden spoon or food processor and beat until light and fluffy.

- Eggs should be added one at a time and, to prevent curdling, each should be beaten in well before the next is added.

- Always sift dry ingredients before using, as this helps incorporate air and gives a lighter result.

- Sponge cakes depend for their lightness on the air beaten into the eggs and sugar, so when adding flour to a sponge mixture, fold it in, do not beat, and cease as soon as all the dry flour has been absorbed.

- Never put wet fruit into a cake — always dry it or mix it with a little of the flour mixture to prevent it sinking to the bottom.

- Press rich fruit cake mixture firmly into the corners of the tin in order to get a good shape. Cover the cake with greaseproof paper if it begins to brown too quickly during cooking.

- Test the cake near the end of the recommended baking time to see if it is cooked through. If pressed lightly with a fingertip most cakes should spring back immediately when cooked. Very rich cakes and chocolate cakes, however, may dent slightly and still be done. Alternatively, insert a wooden skewer gently into the centre of the cake; if it comes out clean, then the cake is ready.

- Always remove cakes from the oven after baking and allow to cool.

The language of cake-making

TO BEAT: vigorous mixing with a spoon or electric mixer.

TO BLEND: combine one ingredient with another until
completely mixed together, either using a fork, wooden
spoon or electric mixer.

TO CREAM: usually refers to butter or fat, alone or
mixed with sugar until light, pale yellow and fluffy.

TO FOLD: carefully incorporate one mixture into another
— usually a light one such as whipped egg whites into
a heavier mixture. Folding involves gently 'drawing' a
figure of eight with a metal spoon and being careful
not to knock the air out of the lighter mixture.

TO STIR: mix carefully in a circular motion to combine.

TO WHIP: beat rapidly with a whisk or electric mixer to incorporate as much air as possible. Cream or egg whites are examples of ingredients that are whipped.

TO BAKE BLIND: precook pastry by lining it with non-stick baking paper, weighing it down with uncooked rice or dried pulses and baking it in the oven.

TO COOK IN A 'BAIN MARIE' (WATER BATH): the pudding dish is placed in a baking tin filled with hot water reaching halfway up the sides of the dish; this method protects any delicate mixture that requires a gentle, indirect heat.

Almond Cake

150 g butter

1 cup castor sugar

3 eggs

¾ teaspoon almond extract

1½ cups plain flour

3 teaspoons baking powder

70 g ground almonds

¾ cup milk

icing sugar, for dusting

Preheat the oven to 160°C. Lightly grease and flour a 20-cm cake tin.

Cream butter and sugar, then beat in eggs and almond extract. Add sifted flour and baking powder and ground almonds alternately with milk. Mix well.

Pour into cake tin and bake for 50–60 minutes. Leave in tin for 10 minutes before removing. Dust with icing sugar.

Almond Sponge

6 eggs, separated

⅓ cup castor sugar

3 tablespoons orange juice

¼ teaspoon vanilla extract

⅔ cup plain flour

1½ cups ground almonds

1 tablespoon finely grated
 orange zest

pinch of salt

1 teaspoon cream of tartar

⅓ cup castor sugar

fresh berries, for decorating

Preheat the oven to 150°C. Lightly grease and flour a 25-cm bundt pan.

Using an electric mixer, whisk the egg yolks and castor sugar until thick and creamy. Add the orange juice and vanilla extract. Combine the sifted flour, almonds, orange zest and pinch of salt. Fold into the egg-yolk mixture. Whisk the egg whites and cream of tartar until soft peaks form. Slowly whisk in the sugar until glossy. Fold into the cake batter until combined. Pour the batter into the prepared pan. Bake for 45–50 minutes.

Cool in the pan, then invert onto a serving platter and spoon the berries into the middle.

Serve with cream.

Apple, Blackberry & Rhubarb Blanket Pie

1⅓ cups plain flour

125 g butter, cut into small
  pieces

4–5 tablespoons sour cream
  or chilled water

FILLING

400 g rhubarb, trimmed and
  cut into small chunks

250 g apples, peeled, cored
  and cut into small chunks

250 g fresh blackberries or
  mulberries (or defrosted
  frozen berries)

½ cup castor sugar, for
  sprinkling

2 tablespoons milk or egg
  wash for glazing pastry

1 tablespoon castor sugar

Preheat the oven to 200°C. Lightly flour a shallow baking tin or
pizza tray.

Sift the flour into a food processor and add the butter. Process for
1 minute or until the mixture resembles coarse breadcrumbs. Add the
sour cream and pulse until the pastry dough comes together. Remove
and shape into a ball. Chill for 20 minutes while you prepare the filling.

Mix all the fruit together in a bowl and stir in the sugar. Working on
a floured board, roll out the pastry to about 30 cm in diameter. ➤

Using a rolling pin, lift the pastry onto the prepared tin or tray. Spoon the fruit into the middle and carefully bring the pastry up, folding it to make a round free-form shape. Leave a small gap in the centre, exposing some of the fruit.

Brush the pastry with milk and sprinkle over the castor sugar.

Bake for 30–40 minutes or until the pastry is crisp and golden and the fruit is tender. Cool a little before lifting onto a serving plate.

Serve warm with Pouring Custard (see page 215).

SERVES 6

Apple & Cinnamon Cake

1 cup self-raising flour

2 tablespoons castor sugar

3 tablespoons softened butter

1 egg, lightly beaten

1/3 cup milk

TOPPING

200 g green apples, peeled, cored and thinly sliced

1/2 teaspoon ground cinnamon

1 teaspoon cornflour

1½ tablespoons butter, melted

Preheat the oven to 180°C. Lightly grease a 23-cm round springform cake tin and line the base with non-stick baking paper.

Sift the flour and sugar into a mixing bowl. Add the butter and cut into the flour until mixture resembles coarse breadcrumbs. Stir in the egg and milk and beat to a smooth batter. Spread over the base of the prepared tin.

Combine the apple, cinnamon and cornflour in a bowl. Arrange on top of the cake batter. Drizzle melted butter over the top.

Bake for 45 minutes or until cooked through. Cool in the tin on a rack. Remove from the tin when cold.

Apple & Date Ring

1 cup chopped stoned dates

½ cup hot water

1 cup plain flour

1 cup sugar

1 teaspoon baking powder

1 teaspoon bicarbonate of soda

2 eggs

½ cup vegetable oil

2 teaspoons vanilla extract

1½ cups grated apple

TOPPING

1 cup desiccated coconut

¼ cup sugar

1 egg

Preheat the oven to 180°C. Lightly grease and flour a 20-cm ring tin.

Place chopped dates in saucepan with water and bring to boil. Remove from heat and leave to stand for 15 minutes. Sift flour, sugar, baking powder and bicarbonate of soda together. Beat eggs lightly with oil and vanilla extract. Add to dry ingredients, together with chopped dates and apple. Mix until just combined.

Pour into ring tin and bake for 30–35 minutes, or until cake springs back when lightly touched. Remove from oven and increase temperature to 190°C.

To make coconut topping, beat coconut, sugar and egg together. Spread over cake and bake for a further 10 minutes or until golden. Allow to cool in tin before turning onto a rack.

Apple & Orange Pudding

1 kg Granny Smith apples, peeled, cored and cut into chunks

grated zest and juice of 1 orange

¼ cup brown sugar

TOPPING

100 g softened butter

100 g brown sugar

2 large eggs

1 teaspoon baking powder

1 cup self-raising flour, sifted

50 g flaked almonds, for decorating

Preheat the oven to 180°C. Lightly grease a 2-litre ovenproof dish.

Combine the apple, orange zest and juice, and brown sugar in the ovenproof dish.

Place all the topping ingredients in an electric mixer and beat slowly until combined. Beat on high speed until soft and fluffy (about 1 minute).

Spoon the topping over the apple to cover it, spreading the mixture to the edges. Sprinkle the flaked almonds over the top.

Bake for 35–40 minutes or until lightly browned on top.

Serve immediately with ice-cream or cream.

SERVES 4

Apple, Rum & Date Cake

½ cup chopped stoned dates,
  soaked in ¼ cup rum

140 g butter

1½ cups castor sugar

3 eggs

2 cups self-raising flour

½ teaspoon ground nutmeg

½ teaspoon ground cinnamon

½ teaspoon ground ginger

½ teaspoon ground cloves

pinch of salt

1 teaspoon baking powder

2 cups chopped walnuts

2 cups peeled, cored and
  chopped apples

Preheat the oven to 180°C. Lightly grease a 23-cm springform cake tin and line the base with non-stick baking paper.

Place the chopped dates and rum in a small saucepan. Cook for 5 minutes over a gentle heat. Remove and cool.

Cream the butter and sugar in a mixing bowl until light and fluffy. Add the eggs one at a time until well combined.

Sift all the dry ingredients into a mixing bowl. Coat the chopped walnut and apple with a little flour. Fold the dry ingredients, then the walnut and apple into the butter mixture. Stir through the chopped date mixture.

Pour into the prepared tin and bake for 60–75 minutes or until cooked through. Cool in the tin and then turn out onto a rack. Serve with whipped cream.

Apricot Almond Cake

1½ cups chopped dried apricots

2 cups orange juice

125 g butter

½ cup brown sugar

½ cup honey

1 egg

1½ cups plain flour

½ teaspoon bicarbonate of soda

2 teaspoons baking powder

1½ cups wholemeal flour

1 cup chopped almonds

¼ cup blanched whole almonds

Preheat the oven to 180°C. Lightly grease a 20-cm round tin and line the base with non-stick baking paper.

Soak chopped apricot in orange juice overnight. Cream butter, brown sugar and honey until light and fluffy. Add egg, beating well. Sift plain flour, bicarbonate of soda and baking powder into large bowl, add wholemeal flour and chopped almonds. Fold flour mixture into creamed mixture, then fold in chopped apricot.

Pour into tin and arrange whole almonds over the top. Bake for 60–80 minutes.

Arabian Date & Nut Cake

¾ cup hot strong coffee

1 cup chopped stoned dates

½ cup chopped walnuts

125 g butter

1 cup sugar

2 eggs

1¾ cups plain flour

½ teaspoon bicarbonate
   of soda

½ teaspoon salt

1½ teaspoons baking powder

1 teaspoon vanilla extract

pinch of salt

icing sugar, for dusting

Preheat the oven to 180°C. Lightly grease a 25-cm × 15-cm loaf tin and line the base with non-stick baking paper.

Pour hot coffee over chopped dates and walnuts and allow to cool. Cream butter and sugar, add eggs and beat well. Sift in dry ingredients. Lastly mix in date and nut mixture and vanilla extract.

Pour into prepared cake tin and bake for 50–60 minutes. Dust with icing sugar.

Baked Date Pudding

TOPPING

2 tablespoons butter, melted

4 tablespoons brown sugar

PUDDING

2 eggs

¾ cup brown sugar

1½ cups plain flour

1½ teaspoons baking powder

pinch salt

125 g chopped stoned dates

2 tablespoons chopped walnuts

⅓ cup milk

Preheat the oven to 180°C.

Combine topping ingredients and spread evenly over the bottom of a 20-cm cake tin.

In a bowl standing in a sink of hot water, beat eggs and brown sugar until doubled in volume and light, white and fluffy. Stir in sifted dry ingredients, dates, walnuts and milk. Pour over topping.

Bake in a bain marie (see page xii) for 60 minutes or until pudding comes away from sides. Turn pudding out onto a serving plate so that topping shows uppermost.

Serve sliced in wedges with custard, whipped cream or ice-cream.

SERVES 6

Baked Rice Pudding with Lemon

⅓ cup short-grain rice

½ cup castor sugar

1 litre milk

1 tablespoon butter

finely grated zest of 1 lemon

Preheat the oven to 175°C. Grease a 2-litre ovenproof dish.

Sprinkle the rice over the bottom of the prepared dish. Combine the sugar and milk and pour over the rice. Dot the top with butter.

Bake for 60 minutes. Stir in the lemon zest and bake for a further 15–20 minutes. Allow to stand for 10 minutes.

Serve warm with cream.

SERVES 6

Baked Roly Poly with Hot Jam Sauce

1½ cups self-raising flour

½ cup plain flour

3 tablespoons softened butter

¾ cup buttermilk

6 tablespoons strawberry jam

SAUCE

3 tablespoons blackberry jam

finely grated zest and juice
of 1 large orange

Preheat the oven to 175°C. Lightly grease a shallow baking dish.

Sift the flours into a mixing bowl. Add the butter and rub together until the mixture resembles fine breadcrumbs. Slowly pour in the buttermilk until the mixture comes together and forms a sticky dough.

On a floured board, roll out the dough to approximately 25 cm × 20 cm. Spread the jam over the dough, leaving a border around the edges. Roll up evenly from the short side. Wrap the roll in non-stick baking paper and place in the prepared dish. Bake for 40–45 minutes or until golden.

To make the hot jam sauce, heat the jam, orange zest and juice together over a gentle heat until well combined. Spoon over the roly poly and serve immediately.

SERVES 6

Baked Stuffed Peaches

¾ cup ground almonds

6 amaretti biscuits (almond
   macaroons), crushed

2 tablespoons castor sugar

1 large egg, lightly beaten

½ cup ricotta cheese

6 large, ripe, firm peaches, cut
   in half and stones removed

½ cup white wine

¼ cup orange juice

1 tablespoon butter

Preheat the oven to 180°C. Lightly grease a shallow ovenproof dish.

Combine the almonds, crushed biscuits and sugar. Stir in the egg
and ricotta cheese. Mix to form a sticky ball. Spoon into the cavities
of the halved peaches.

Place in the prepared dish and pour the wine and orange juice over
the top. Dot the top of each peach with butter.

Bake for 25–30 minutes or until lightly browned on top.

Serve warm or cold with ice-cream or Pouring Custard (see page 215).

SERVES 6

Banana Bread Pudding

½ cup orange marmalade

5 thick slices white bread

3 large bananas, peeled and cut
  into thick slices

4 large eggs, lightly beaten

1 litre milk

2 cups sugar

2 teaspoons vanilla extract

1 teaspoon ground nutmeg

1 tablespoon ground cinnamon

4 tablespoons butter, melted

icing sugar, for dusting

Preheat the oven to 180°C. Lightly grease a 2-litre ovenproof dish.

Spread the marmalade on the bread slices and then cut the bread into small chunks. Lay half of the bread chunks over the base of the prepared dish. Arrange the banana slices over the bread and then place the remainder of the bread chunks on the top.

Combine the eggs, milk, sugar, vanilla extract and spices. Whisk in the melted butter. Pour the mixture over the bread and banana.

Cover the dish with foil and place into a bain marie (see page xii). Bake for 30 minutes. Remove the foil and bake for a further 30 minutes or until the pudding is firm and lightly browned on top.

Remove from the baking dish and cool a little. Dust with icing sugar before serving.

SERVES 8

Banana & Buttermilk Cake

200 g unsalted butter

1 cup castor sugar

3 large eggs

1 cup mashed banana

2 teaspoons vanilla extract

1 cup buttermilk

1¾ cups self-raising flour

1 teaspoon bicarbonate of soda

pinch of salt

Preheat the oven to 180°C. Lightly grease a 23-cm springform cake tin and line the base with non-stick baking paper.

Cream the butter and sugar until light and fluffy. Add the eggs, mashed banana, vanilla extract and buttermilk. Sift the flour, bicarbonate of soda and salt into another bowl. Stir the flour mixture into the batter and mix until smooth.

Pour into the prepared tin and bake for 45 minutes or until cooked through.

Cool in the tin for 10 minutes. Turn out onto a rack and cool for 10 minutes more.

Serve warm with Butterscotch Sauce (see page 213).

Banana & Fresh Fig Gratin

4 fresh figs, quartered

4 ripe, firm bananas, peeled and
  thickly sliced

3 eggs

1½ tablespoons ground almonds

1 teaspoon vanilla extract

300 ml cream

¼ cup brown sugar

icing sugar, for dusting

Preheat the oven to 180°C. Lightly grease a square 1-litre ovenproof
dish and place the fruit in the bottom.

Beat the eggs, ground almonds, vanilla extract, cream and brown sugar.
Pour over the fruit.

Place on a preheated baking tray and bake for 10–15 minutes or until
nearly set.

Place under a hot grill until lightly browned.

Dust liberally with icing sugar before serving warm.

SERVES 4

Banana Layer Cake

65 g butter

½ cup sugar

2 eggs, beaten

2 tablespoons milk

1 cup mashed banana

1⅓ cups self-raising
  wholemeal flour

FILLING

125 g butter

1 egg white

¾ cup demerara sugar

1 teaspoon liqueur

2 bananas, sliced

Preheat the oven to 200°C. Grease and flour two sandwich tins.

Cream butter and sugar, and add beaten eggs gradually. Combine milk and mashed banana and add to mixture alternately with sifted flour.

Pour into prepared tins and bake for 25 minutes.

To make butter cream filling, cream butter thoroughly, and add whisked egg white by the spoonful. Beat in sugar gradually and flavour with liqueur.

Sandwich cake halves together with butter cream and sliced bananas and decorate top of cake in the same way.

Banana Mousse Pie

PASTRY

100 g chilled butter

1½ cups plain flour

1 teaspoon grated lemon zest

50 g icing sugar

1 egg, lightly beaten

2–3 tablespoons chilled water

FILLING

4 ripe bananas, peeled

½ cup brown sugar

2 tablespoons rum

3 eggs, separated

TOPPING

2 ripe bananas, peeled

½ cup flaked almonds

2 tablespoons castor sugar

icing sugar, for dusting

Pulse the butter and flour in a food processor until the mixture resembles fine breadcrumbs. Add the lemon zest and icing sugar and pulse for 1 minute.

Combine the egg and water and, with the motor running, slowly pour enough liquid into the food processor to draw the mixture together. Remove and roll into a ball. Chill for 30 minutes.

Preheat the oven to 200°C. Lightly grease a 20-cm pie dish. **>**

On a floured board, roll out the pastry and fit into the prepared dish, cutting away any excess. Blind-bake the pastry shell (see page xii) on a preheated baking tray for 10–15 minutes or until lightly browned at the sides.

Reduce the oven temperature to 175°C.

In a food processor, blend four bananas with the brown sugar, rum and egg yolks until smooth. Whip the egg whites until stiff. Carefully fold through the banana mixture. Pour into the prebaked pastry case. Slice the remaining two bananas over the top of the pie and bake for 20 minutes or until firm.

Sprinkle with flaked almonds and castor sugar.

Preheat the grill until hot and grill the pie for 2–3 minutes to caramelise the nutty topping.

Serve warm or cold dusted with icing sugar.

SERVES 6

Banana Sherry Cake

125 g butter

¾ cup sugar

2 eggs

1 teaspoon vanilla extract

3 bananas, mashed

1½ cups plain flour

1½ teaspoons baking powder

½ teaspoon salt

½ teaspoon bicarbonate of soda

1 tablespoon milk

TOPPING

½ teaspoon gelatine powder

2 teaspoons water

⅔ cup cream

2 teaspoons icing sugar

1 teaspoon sherry

chopped walnuts or grated
    dark chocolate for decorating

Preheat the oven to 180°C. Lightly grease and flour a 23-cm cake tin.

Cream butter and sugar, then beat in eggs and add vanilla. Fold in mashed banana. Add sifted flour, baking powder and salt. Dissolve bicarbonate of soda in milk and stir into flour mixture.

Pour into the prepared cake tin and bake for 30–35 minutes. Turn onto a rack to cool.

To make sherry cream topping, stir gelatine in water over gentle heat until dissolved. Whisk cream, beat in icing sugar and cooled gelatine. Fold in sherry. Spread over cooled cake and sprinkle with nuts or chocolate.

Banana Walnut Cake

125 g butter

1 cup castor sugar

2 eggs

1 cup mashed banana

1 teaspoon vanilla extract

2¼ cups self-raising flour

¼ teaspoon bicarbonate of soda

½ cup water

TOPPING

50 g softened butter

2 tablespoons self-raising flour

2 tablespoons sugar

1 teaspoon ground cinnamon

2 tablespoons chopped walnuts

Preheat the oven to 180°C. Lightly grease a 23-cm square tin and line the base with non-stick baking paper.

Cream butter and sugar until light and fluffy. Add eggs one at a time, beating well after each addition. Add banana and vanilla extract, and beat well. Sift flour and bicarbonate of soda and add to creamed mixture with water.

Pour into prepared tin.

To make topping, rub butter into flour, add remaining ingredients and mix well.

Place topping over cake mixture and bake for 40–45 minutes.

Berry Cake

1 cup plain flour

100 g butter, melted

1 egg

½ cup sugar

1½ teaspoons baking powder

1 teaspoon vanilla extract

3 cups fresh or frozen berries
(blackberries, blueberries,
raspberries)

TOPPING

2 cups sour cream

½ cup sugar

1½ tablespoons custard
powder

2 egg yolks

1 teaspoon vanilla extract

Preheat the oven to 180°C. Lightly grease and flour a 23-cm springform tin.

Mix together all cake ingredients except berries. Pour into prepared tin. Cover with berries.

Beat topping ingredients together and pour on top of berries. Bake for 50–60 minutes.

Serve with whipped cream and fruit.

Black Bottom Cake

225 g cream cheese

1 egg

1⅓ cups sugar

pinch of salt

175 g dark chocolate chips

1½ cups flour

1 teaspoon bicarbonate of soda

½ cup cocoa

½ teaspoon salt

100 g butter, melted

1 cup water

1 teaspoon vanilla extract

1 tablespoon vinegar

ICING

65 g dark cooking chocolate

⅔ cup cream

Preheat the oven to 190°C. Lightly grease and flour a 20-cm cake tin.

Beat together cream cheese, egg, a quarter of the sugar and a pinch of salt. Stir in chocolate chips. Into another bowl sift flour, bicarbonate of soda, cocoa and salt, then add remaining sugar, melted butter, water, vanilla extract and vinegar.

Pour flour mixture into prepared cake tin. Spread cream cheese mixture on top. Bake for 45 minutes. Allow to cool before removing from tin.

To make chocolate icing, melt together chocolate and cream and pour over cake.

Blueberry & Ricotta Cake

60 g butter, melted

½ cup castor sugar

1 egg

¾ cup sour cream

½ teaspoon vanilla extract

1 cup self-raising flour

TOPPING

1 cup icing sugar

225 g ricotta cheese

1 egg

2 tablespoons freshly squeezed lemon juice

2 cups fresh blueberries

Preheat the oven to 180°C. Lightly grease and flour a 22-cm springform cake tin.

Using an electric mixer, beat the butter, sugar and egg together for about 1 minute until pale and thick. Mix in the sour cream, vanilla extract and sifted flour.

Spoon the batter into the prepared tin and bake for 20 minutes or until lightly browned and risen.

To make topping, beat the icing sugar, ricotta, egg and lemon juice together until smooth. Pour onto the hot cake and sprinkle the blueberries over the top. Return to the oven and bake for a further 30 minutes or until the cake topping is set and lightly browned. Cool in the tin on a rack.

Serve warm or at room temperature.

Brandy Apple Spice Cake

1 cup raisins

¾ cup brandy

4 cups peeled, cored and
    chopped Granny Smith apples

2 cups raw sugar

½ cup vegetable oil

2 eggs

2 cups plain flour

2 teaspoons bicarbonate of soda

1 teaspoon salt

2 teaspoons ground cinnamon

1 teaspoon freshly grated
    nutmeg

¼ teaspoon ground cloves

1 cup chopped walnuts

Preheat the oven to 160°C. Lightly grease and flour a 23-cm square fluted flan tin or 23-cm springform tin.

Soak raisins in brandy for 2 hours to plump them, add apple and mix well. Beat sugar, oil and eggs until pale and creamy. Sift flour, bicarbonate of soda, salt and spices into oil mixture. Add apple mixture and chopped walnuts, combining well.

Pour into prepared tin. Bake for 90 minutes.

Allow to cool in tin before turning onto a wire rack. Serve with whipped cream.

Brown Walnut Cake

75 g butter

125 g sugar

2 eggs, beaten

1½ cups plain flour

1 teaspoon ground ginger

1 teaspoon ground cinnamon

1 teaspoon bicarbonate of soda

¾ cup milk

⅓ cup golden syrup

1 cup chopped walnuts

icing sugar, for dusting

Preheat the oven to 180°C. Lightly grease and flour a 20-cm cake tin.

Cream butter and sugar, and add beaten eggs. Stir in sifted flour and spices. Fold in chopped walnuts. Dissolve bicarbonate of soda in milk and add to mixture. Warm golden syrup and mix in.

Pour into prepared tin and bake for 40–45 minutes, or until cooked. Dust with icing sugar or ice as required.

Caramel Cake

125 g butter

1 cup sugar

1 egg

1½ cups plain flour

½ teaspoon salt

1 teaspoon baking powder

1 tablespoon golden syrup

1 cup milk

1 teaspoon bicarbonate of soda

½ cup raisins

1 tablespoon cocoa

Preheat the oven to 200°C. Lightly grease and flour a 23-cm cake tin.

Cream butter and sugar, and beat in egg. Sift flour, salt and baking powder into a separate bowl. Melt golden syrup and milk, and add bicarbonate of soda. Add milk mixture and sifted dry ingredients alternately to the creamed mixture.

Pour half the mixture into prepared cake tin. Sprinkle over raisins. Stir cocoa into remaining mixture. Pour this on top of raisins. Bake for 35–40 minutes. Ice with Chocolate Icing (see page 213).

Carol's Very Moist Carrot Cake

2 cups plain flour

2 teaspoons bicarbonate of soda

2 teaspoons baking powder

2 teaspoons ground cinnamon

1 teaspoon salt

2 cups castor sugar

1 cup chopped walnuts

1½ cups vegetable oil

4 eggs

3 cups grated peeled carrot

chopped walnuts, for decorating

Preheat the oven to 175°C. Line a 23-cm square cake tin with non-stick baking paper.

Sift the flour into a large mixing bowl with the bicarbonate of soda, baking powder, cinnamon and salt. Stir in the sugar and chopped walnuts. In another bowl, mix the oil and eggs until well combined. Stir in the grated carrot.

Pour the wet mixture into the dry ingredients and mix to form a smooth batter. Pour into the prepared tin and bake for 60–80 minutes or until cooked through. Cool for 5 minutes before turning out onto a rack.

When completely cold, use a spatula to cover the top and sides of the cake with Cream Cheese Icing (see page 214) and decorate with chopped walnuts.

Cherry & Pineapple Ring

175 g butter

175 g castor sugar

2 eggs, beaten

1½ cups self-raising flour

3 tablespoons milk

65 g glacé cherries, quartered

25 g glacé pineapple, chopped

glacé pineapple and glacé cherries,
   for decorating

Preheat the oven to 180°C. Lightly grease a 20-cm ring tin and line
the base with non-stick baking paper.

Cream butter and sugar. Add eggs a little at a time, beating well after each
addition and adding 1 tablespoon sifted flour with last amount of egg. Fold
remaining sifted flour into mixture, then add milk, cherries and pineapple.

Pour into prepared tin and bake for 55–60 minutes. Turn out onto a rack.
Ice when cool with Glacé Icing (see page 214). Decorate with glacé
pineapple and cherries, trickling any remaining icing over fruit and down
sides of cake.

Cherry & Walnut Cake

175 g butter

175 g sugar

3 eggs, beaten

2 tablespoons milk

½ cup chopped walnuts

few drops lemon essence

50 g glacé cherries, halved

1½ cups plain flour

1 teaspoon baking powder

desiccated coconut and glacé
    cherries, for decorating

Preheat the oven to 180°C. Lightly grease and flour a 20-cm cake tin.

Cream butter and sugar, add eggs, milk, chopped walnuts, lemon essence, glacé cherries, and sifted flour and baking powder.

Pour into prepared tin and bake for 60–90 minutes, or until cooked.

Ice with Lemon Icing (see page 214), sprinkle with coconut and decorate with glacé cherries.

Chilled Summer Berry Pudding

1 kg mixed fresh or frozen berries (stoned cherries,
   raspberries, blueberries, blackberries, strawberries,
   mulberries)

1 cup castor sugar

100 ml fresh orange juice

10–12 thin slices of white, day-old bread, crusts removed

Combine the fruit, sugar and orange juice in a saucepan. Cook over
a gentle heat for 4–5 minutes or until the sugar has melted and the
fruit juices start to flow. Remove and cool a little.

Line a 1.7-litre pudding basin with the sliced bread, cutting it to neatly
fit the sides and base. Spoon in about two-thirds of the fruit and leave
for 30 minutes. Spoon in the remaining fruit and cover the top with bread
slices so that the fruit is completely enclosed. Place a piece of plastic
film or non-stick baking paper over the top and then place a plate on top
of the pudding to weigh it down. Refrigerate overnight.

Remove the plate and loosen the sides with a palate knife before turning
the pudding out onto a deep-sided serving plate, to catch any excess
fruit juices.

Serve in slices with ice-cream or cream.

SERVES 8

Chocolate Cherry Clafoutis

450 g black cherries, stoned   50 g icing sugar

4 tablespoons brandy or rum   25 g butter, melted

½ cup plain flour   300 ml milk

2 tablespoons cocoa   3 eggs, lightly beaten

pinch of salt   icing sugar, for dusting

Preheat the oven to 220°C. Generously grease a 1-litre ovenproof dish. Soak the cherries in the brandy or rum for 20 minutes.

Make the batter in a food processor by first sifting the flour, cocoa, salt and icing sugar together. With the motor running, pour in the melted butter, milk and eggs and blend to a smooth batter.

Pour about half a cup of the batter into the base of the prepared dish and bake for 10 minutes or until just set.

Drain any liquid from the cherries and mix it into the reserved batter. Spoon the cherries over the base of the baking dish and then pour the remaining batter over the fruit.

Bake for 40–45 minutes or until risen and set. Leave to cool for 5 minutes. Dust generously with icing sugar. Serve warm with cream or ice-cream.

SERVES 4

Chocolate Chip Cake

200 g softened butter

200 g castor sugar

3 eggs, lightly beaten

275 g self-raising flour

150 g dark chocolate chips, or roughly
   chopped dark cooking chocolate

50 g ground almonds

2 tablespoons milk

25 g chopped almonds

Preheat the oven to 180°C. Lightly grease a 20-cm round springform cake tin and line the base with non-stick baking paper.

Cream the butter and sugar until light and fluffy. Add the eggs a little at a time, alternating with a tablespoon of flour. Beat well to make a light batter. Fold in the remaining flour, chocolate, ground almonds and milk. Sprinkle the chopped almonds over the top.

Pour the mixture into the prepared tin and bake for 90 minutes or until cooked through. Cool in the tin for 5 minutes before turning out onto a rack.

Chocolate Fudge Cake

125 g butter

¾ cup brown sugar

1 tablespoon cocoa

1 egg, lightly beaten

2 tablespoons desiccated coconut

½ cup chopped walnuts, or sunflower
   or sesame seeds

¼ cup chopped morella stoned cherries

½ cup sultanas

½ teaspoon vanilla extract

2 cups crushed Marie biscuits or other sweet biscuits

Lightly grease a 20-cm × 30-cm tin and line the base with non-stick baking paper.

In a large saucepan melt butter, sugar and cocoa. Remove from heat and add egg and remaining ingredients. Combine well.

Press into prepared tin and refrigerate until firm.

Ice with Chocolate Icing (see page 213). Store in refrigerator.

Chocolate, Hazelnut & Ricotta Cheesecake

BASE

50 g finely chopped hazelnuts

100 g sweet biscuit crumbs

75 g butter, melted

FILLING

2 eggs, separated

35 g castor sugar

¾ cup ricotta cheese

20 g ground hazelnuts

75 ml cream

1 tablespoon cocoa

1 teaspoon dark rum

icing sugar, for dusting

Preheat the oven to 170°C. Lightly grease a 20-cm springform cake tin and line the base with non-stick baking paper.

Combine the base ingredients and press into the base of the prepared tin.

Whisk the egg yolks and sugar until thick and creamy. Beat in the ricotta, ground hazelnuts, cream and cocoa. Stir in the dark rum.

Whip the egg whites until stiff and carefully fold through the chocolate mixture. Pour into the prepared tin and bake for 60 minutes or until lightly risen and just firm to touch.

Cool a little before removing from the tin. Dust liberally with icing sugar before serving.

Chocolate Mousse Cake

225 g dark cooking chocolate,
    chopped

125 g unsalted butter

7 eggs, separated

½ cup castor sugar

3 tablespoons brandy

pinch of salt

icing sugar, for dusting

Preheat the oven to 160°C. Lightly grease a 23-cm springform cake tin and line the base with non-stick baking paper.

Place the chocolate and butter in a bowl, set over a saucepan of simmering water and stir until melted. Remove and cool a little.

Using an electric mixer, beat the egg yolks and sugar until pale and thick (3–4 minutes). Stir in the cooled chocolate mixture and brandy. In another bowl, whip the egg whites with a pinch of salt until stiff. Take two large spoonfuls of the egg-white mixture and carefully mix this through the chocolate mixture. Tip the chocolate mixture into the egg-white mixture and fold through.

Spoon into the prepared tin and bake for 30–35 minutes or until cooked.

Cool in the tin on a rack. The cake will fall in the centre a little. When cold, remove from the tin and turn out onto a plate. Dust with icing sugar.

Chocolate Pudding Cake

1½ cups water

1 cup raisins

250 g butter

1 cup sugar

½ teaspoon ground cinnamon

½ teaspoon ground ginger

½ teaspoon ground mixed spice

3 tablespoons cocoa

pinch of salt

1 teaspoon bicarbonate of
soda dissolved in ¼ cup
boiling water

2 cups plain flour

Preheat the oven to 180°C. Lightly grease a 23-cm round or oval cake tin and line the base with non-stick baking paper.

Combine the water, raisins, butter, sugar, spices, cocoa and salt in a saucepan. Gently heat until boiling and then turn down to a simmer and cook for 5 minutes. Remove from the heat and allow to cool. Stir in the bicarbonate of soda mixture. Fold in the sifted flour to make a smooth cake batter.

Pour into the prepared tin and bake for 35–40 minutes or until firm and cooked through. Cool in the tin before turning out onto a rack.

Serve warm with Butterscotch Sauce or Pouring Custard (see pages 213 and 215).

Chocolate & Walnut Caramel Custard Pudding

1 cup sugar

⅓ cup water

30 g dark cooking chocolate

¾ cup toasted walnuts

415-g can sweetened condensed milk

425 ml milk

2 eggs, plus 2 egg yolks

grated chocolate, for decorating

Preheat the oven to 175°C. Lightly grease eight 125-ml custard cups.

Combine the sugar and water in a small saucepan stirring continually until the sugar dissolves. Increase the heat and boil until the sugar syrup starts to turn a golden brown. Immediately remove from the heat and spoon the caramel evenly into eight custard cups.

Process the chocolate and walnuts in a food processor for 1–2 minutes. Transfer to a mixing bowl. Heat the condensed milk and milk in a saucepan until boiling. Pour over the chocolate and nuts. Stir until smooth. Cool slightly, then stir in the eggs and egg yolks.

Spoon the chocolate mixture evenly into the cups. Place the cups in a bain marie (see page xii). Bake for 45 minutes or until the puddings are just set. Take cups out of the bain marie. Cool on a rack. Run a knife around the edge of the puddings and turn out onto serving plates.

Decorate with grated chocolate.

SERVES 8

Chocolate Yoghurt Cake

130 g dark cooking chocolate, chopped

¼ cup water

½ cup yoghurt

50 g butter

½ cup sugar

¼ cup brown sugar

2 small eggs

1 cup plain flour

1 teaspoon bicarbonate of soda

½ teaspoon salt

1 teaspoon vanilla extract

TOPPING

70 g dark cooking chocolate, chopped

¼ cup yoghurt

Preheat the oven to 180°C. Lightly grease and flour a 23-cm ring tin.

Melt chocolate with water, allow to cool and add yoghurt. Cream butter and sugars, then beat in eggs. Sift flour, bicarbonate of soda and salt. Add vanilla extract and sifted ingredients to creamed mixture alternately with yoghurt mixture.

Pour into prepared tin and bake for 35 minutes. Cool.

Prepare topping by melting chocolate and adding yoghurt. Spread over cake.

Classic Orange & Almond Cake

2 whole, thin-skinned oranges

6 eggs

250 g castor sugar

2 cups ground almonds

1 teaspoon baking powder

Preheat the oven to 180°C. Lightly grease a 24-cm round cake tin and line the base with non-stick baking paper.

Place the oranges in a saucepan of cold water and cover. Bring to the boil and cook at a simmer for 2 hours (or until soft). Cool and blend to a pulp in a food processor.

Beat the eggs until fluffy, adding the sugar slowly until a thick, pale mousse-like mixture forms. Carefully fold in the ground almonds and baking powder. Stir in the pulped oranges.

Pour the batter into the prepared tin and bake for 35–40 minutes or until cooked through. Cool in the tin before turning out.

Serve with fresh orange slices, chopped dates and plain creamy yoghurt.

Classic Sponge Pudding
with Strawberry Jam Sauce

100 g softened butter

100 g castor sugar

2 eggs, beaten

175 g self-raising flour

1 teaspoon vanilla extract

3–4 tablespoons milk

SAUCE

⅓ cup strawberry jam

2 tablespoons castor sugar

juice of 1 lemon

2 tablespoons water

Preheat the oven to 190°C. Lightly butter a 900-ml pudding basin or four 200-ml ramekins.

Cream the butter and sugar until light and fluffy. Slowly add the eggs. Fold in the sifted flour, vanilla and milk to make a soft batter that drops off the spoon easily.

Pour into the prepared pudding basin and place in a bain marie (see page xii). Cover tightly with a double thickness of greased foil, pleated in the centre to allow for expansion of the mixture. Bake for 60–90 minutes. Reduce the cooking time to 35–45 minutes for the individual puddings. Remove and turn out.

To make the strawberry jam sauce, place all the ingredients in a saucepan and stir over a gentle heat until smooth. Bring to the boil and cook for 2 minutes. Strain into a jug, and serve with the pudding.

SERVES 4

Coconut Cake
with Caramel Rum Sauce

1 cup castor sugar

120 g softened butter

1 teaspoon vanilla extract

2 eggs

1 cup self-raising flour

¾ cup sour cream

¾ cup shredded coconut

¼ cup coconut cream

SAUCE

½ cup sugar

2 tablespoons water

1 tablespoon dark rum

2 tablespoons butter

½ cup cream

Preheat the oven to 175°C. Lightly grease a 19-cm square cake tin and line the base with non-stick baking paper.

Cream the sugar, butter and vanilla extract until light and fluffy. Add the eggs, one at a time. Fold in the sifted flour. Stir in the sour cream, shredded coconut and coconut cream. Mix to a smooth batter.

Pour into the prepared tin and bake for 45–55 minutes or until lightly browned and cooked through. Cool in the tin on a rack.

To make the caramel rum sauce, slowly heat the sugar and water in a heavy-based saucepan, stirring until the sugar is melted. Increase the heat and cook until the syrup starts to caramelise, turning a light golden colour. Remove from the heat and stir in the dark rum, butter and cream. Whisk over a low heat until the sauce is smooth. Cool. Pour over cake to serve.

Coconut Pudding
with Passionfruit Sauce

4 large eggs

finely grated zest and juice
    of 2 lemons

200 g castor sugar

1½ cups buttermilk

1 cup desiccated coconut

SAUCE

150 ml passionfruit pulp

50 g castor sugar

zest and juice of 1 orange

Preheat the oven to 160°C. Lightly grease a 1-litre ovenproof dish.

Combine the eggs, lemon zest and juice, castor sugar, buttermilk and desiccated coconut.

Pour into the prepared dish and bake for 45–60 minutes or until firm and lightly golden. Cool completely.

To make passionfruit sauce, heat all ingredients in a small saucepan, stirring until the sugar has melted. Bring to the boil and cook for 1 minute. Remove and strain into a bowl. Allow to cool.

Pour sauce over pudding to serve.

SERVES 6

Country Cake

3⅓ cups plain flour

2 teaspoons baking powder

175 g brown sugar

2 teaspoons mixed spice

pinch of ground nutmeg

grated zest of ½ lemon

175 g butter

2 cups raisins

1½ cups currants

¾ cup mixed peel

2 eggs, beaten

½ cup milk

2 tablespoons golden syrup

½ cup dry stout

Preheat the oven to 160°C. Lightly grease a 27-cm cake tin and line the base with non-stick baking paper.

Sift flour, baking powder, sugar, mixed spice and nutmeg into a bowl. Add lemon zest, then rub in butter. Add fruit and peel, make well in centre and pour in eggs, milk and golden syrup. Mix well. Stir in enough stout to make a dropping consistency.

Turn into the prepared tin and bake for 2 hours, or until cooked.

Cut-and-come-again Cake

225 g self-raising flour

pinch of salt

½ teaspoon mixed spice

125 g butter

125 g sugar

125 g chopped raisins

125 g currants

¼ cup mixed peel

1 egg

¼ cup milk

icing sugar, for dusting

Preheat the oven to 180°C. Lightly grease and flour a 20-cm × 10-cm loaf tin.

Sift flour, salt and spice together, then rub in butter. Add sugar, raisins, currants and peel. Beat egg in milk and add to other ingredients, mixing well.

Pour into prepared tin and bake for 60–90 minutes, or until cooked. Dust with icing sugar or ice as required.

Easy Cherry & Ricotta Cheese Strudel

2 cups ricotta cheese

2 eggs, lightly beaten

½ cup stoned tinned cherries, well drained

50 g soft cream cheese

½ cup dried breadcrumbs

3 tablespoons castor sugar

4 sheets filo pastry

50 g butter, melted

icing sugar, for dusting

Preheat the oven to 200°C.

Combine the ricotta, eggs, cherries, cream cheese, dried breadcrumbs and sugar. Chill until ready to use.

Place a sheet of non-stick baking paper on a bench. Lay down the first sheet of filo pastry, shortest side towards you, and brush lightly with melted butter. Lay a second sheet of filo pastry over the top and brush with butter. Repeat with the third and fourth sheets.

Spoon the filling in a thick sausage along the short side of the pastry sheets, leaving a border at the end and on the long sides. Fold the long sides in over the filling. Carefully roll up the filo from the short side to form a log-shaped packet.

Slide onto a baking tray. Sprinkle with icing sugar and bake for 15 minutes.

Reduce the oven temperature to 180°C and bake for a further 15–20 minutes or until the pastry is brown and crisp.

Cool a little before cutting with a serrated knife. Dust with icing sugar before serving.

SERVES 6

English Sherry Trifle

1 small, plain sponge cake

2–3 tablespoons strawberry or raspberry jam

1½ cups medium dry sherry

8 amaretti biscuits (almond macaroons), crushed

1 cup cream

2 cups vanilla custard

2 tablespoons toasted flaked almonds

Cut the cake in half and spread the jam between the layers. Cut into small chunks to fit into the bottom of an attractive glass bowl or dish. Pour the sherry over the top and set aside for 30 minutes.

Sprinkle with the crushed amaretti biscuits. Whip the cream until stiff and mix half of it carefully through the custard. Pour the custard mixture over the sponge and biscuits. Using a piping bag, pipe the rest of the cream to decorate the top. Sprinkle the toasted flaked almonds over the top.

Refrigerate for an hour before serving.

SERVES 6–8

Espresso Coffee & Walnut Cake

125 g icing sugar

4 eggs, separated

1 tablespoon fresh breadcrumbs

1 tablespoon finely ground
  espresso coffee beans

1 tablespoon cocoa

1½ cups walnuts, roughly
  chopped

icing sugar, for dusting

Preheat the oven to 180°C. Lightly grease a 20-cm round springform cake tin and line the base with non-stick baking paper.

Using an electric mixer beat the icing sugar and egg yolks until pale and thick. Stir in the breadcrumbs, coffee beans, cocoa and chopped walnuts.

In another bowl, whip the egg whites until stiff. Fold two large spoonfuls of the coffee batter into the egg whites. Tip the egg-white mixture into the remaining coffee batter and fold carefully with a spoon.

Pour the batter into the prepared tin and bake for 55–60 minutes or until cooked through. Cool in the tin before carefully turning out onto a serving plate.

Dust with icing sugar and serve with whipped cream.

Fairy Cakes

125 g butter
⅔ cup castor sugar
2 eggs
1 cup plain flour
2 teaspoons baking powder
1½ tablespoons milk

Preheat the oven to 190°C. Lay out 24 fairy cake papers on a baking tray.

Cream butter and sugar until light and fluffy. Add eggs one at a time, beating well after each addition. Sift flour and baking powder into mixture and add milk. Mix thoroughly but do not beat.

Place a large teaspoonful of mixture in each paper case. Bake for 15–20 minutes or until cooked.

Allow to cool before decorating with icing or your favourite filling.

Family Chocolate Cake

125 g softened butter

⅔ cup sugar

½ cup icing sugar

1¼ cups self-raising flour

½ cup cocoa

1 teaspoon bicarbonate of soda

pinch of salt

2 eggs

1 cup milk

1 teaspoon vanilla extract

Preheat the oven to 180°C. Lightly grease and flour a 23-cm cake tin.

Cream butter with sugar and icing sugar. Sift flour, cocoa, bicarbonate of soda and salt into a separate bowl. Add flour mixture to creamed margarine with remaining ingredients and beat well.

Spoon into prepared tin and bake for 40–55 minutes, or until cooked.

Ice with Chocolate Icing (see page 213) when cold.

Fig, Ginger & Pecan Loaf

185 g softened butter

¾ cup castor sugar

3 eggs, lightly beaten

150 g sultanas

150 g glacé figs

150 g glacé ginger

½ cup plain flour

½ cup self-raising flour

⅔ cup pecan nuts, roughly chopped

Preheat the oven to 160°C. Lightly grease a 23-cm × 12-cm loaf pan and line the base with non-stick baking paper.

Cream the butter and sugar until light and fluffy. Slowly add the eggs until combined. Stir in the sultanas, figs and ginger. Sift the flours into another bowl and mix in the nuts. Fold into the cake batter.

Spoon into the prepared pan and bake for 75 minutes or until cooked through. Cool in the tin for 20 minutes before turning out onto a rack.

Fran's Dairy-free Chocolate Cake

3 cups plain flour

½ teaspoon salt

1 teaspoon baking powder

1 teaspoon bicarbonate of soda

⅔ cup cocoa or carob powder

2 cups sugar

2 tablespoons vinegar

2 cups chilled water

⅔ cup vegetable oil

1 teaspoon vanilla extract

Preheat the oven to 180°C. Lightly grease and flour a 23-cm cake tin.

Sift flour, salt, baking powder, bicarbonate of soda and cocoa into large bowl. Add remaining ingredients and mix well.

Pour into prepared tin and bake for 40–45 minutes. Ice with Chocolate Icing (see page 213).

Fresh Plum Tart
with Crumble Topping

1 cup castor sugar

pinch of salt

125 g chilled butter

1¼ cups plain flour

½ teaspoon ground cinnamon

¼ teaspoon baking powder

2 eggs

¼ cup castor sugar

½ cup sour cream

½ teaspoon vanilla extract

12 dark plums, stoned and
each cut into eight

icing sugar, for dusting

Preheat the oven to 180°C. Lightly grease a 20-cm tart tin.

Combine the sugar, salt, butter and flour in a food processor and pulse until the mixture resembles coarse breadcrumbs. Divide the mixture into two. Add the cinnamon and baking powder to one mixture. Lightly beat one egg and stir into the mixture to form a sticky ball. Press into the base of the tart tin and cook for 10 minutes or until just set.

Meanwhile, whisk the other egg with the castor sugar, sour cream and vanilla extract.

Remove the base from the oven and arrange the plums over the top. Pour the egg custard mixture over the plums. Take the remaining flour-and-butter mixture and sprinkle it over the top. ❯

Return to the oven and bake for 20–30 minutes or until lightly browned. Cool a little.

Dust with icing sugar and serve with Pouring Custard (see page 215) or cream.

SERVES 6

Fruity Christmas Pudding

150 g raisins

150 g sultanas

80 g currants

50 g mixed peel

50 g dried apple, chopped

25 g prunes, stoned and roughly chopped

25 g dates, stoned and roughly chopped

50 ml rum

30 ml dark ale

125 g butter

100 g brown sugar

40 g peeled carrot, finely grated

20 g plain flour

40 g finely chopped almonds

1 tablespoon dark treacle

½ teaspoon mixed spice

¼ teaspoon ground nutmeg

1 egg

1¼ cups fresh breadcrumbs

1¼ cups dried breadcrumbs

Combine the dried fruit in a large bowl and pour the rum and dark ale over the top. Leave to soak for a day.

Melt the butter and brown sugar. Pour the mixture over the fruit and stir in the remaining ingredients. Mix well with a spoon or use your hands.

Divide the mixture into half and form into two balls. Place each pudding into a baking bag and tie with string, leaving room for the pudding to swell a little. ➤

Suspend in a pot of simmering water and cook, covered, for 2½ hours. Remove and leave to cool.

To reheat, cook in the bag for 40 minutes or until the pudding is heated through.

Serve warm with ice-cream or Pouring Custard (see page 215) – perhaps with a splash of rum added to it.

SERVES 12 (MAKES TWO 600-g PUDDINGS)

Fruity Yoghurt Cake

1 cup sugar

125 g softened butter

2 eggs

2 cups plain flour

1 teaspoon baking powder

1 teaspoon bicarbonate of soda

pinch of salt

1 cup yoghurt

1 teaspoon vanilla extract

2 teaspoons ground cinnamon

½ cup raisins

½ cup chopped walnuts

icing sugar, for dusting

Preheat the oven to 180°C. Lightly grease and flour a 23-cm square tin.

Cream three-quarters of the sugar with butter until light and fluffy. Add eggs one at a time, beating well after each addition. Sift flour, baking powder, bicarbonate of soda and salt. Stir into creamed mixture alternately with yoghurt until just blended. Stir in vanilla extract.

Pour 2 cups of mixture into prepared tin. Combine remaining sugar, cinnamon, raisins and walnuts, and sprinkle ½ cup over mixture in tin. Stir remaining nut mixture into mixture in bowl. Spread over mixture in tin.

Bake for 45 minutes, or until cooked. Dust with icing sugar.

Ginger & Apple Upside-down Cake

3 tablespoons brown sugar

2 Granny Smith apples, peeled, cored
   and thinly sliced

4 cups plain flour

4 teaspoons ground ginger

225 g butter

2 cups sugar

4 tablespoons golden syrup

2 teaspoons bicarbonate of soda

1½ cups milk

2 tablespoons lemon juice

Preheat the oven to 170°C. Lightly grease a deep 20-cm cake tin and line
with non-stick baking paper.

Sprinkle the lined tin with the brown sugar. Arrange apple slices to cover
bottom of tin. Sift flour and ginger and rub in butter. Add sugar, golden
syrup, and bicarbonate of soda dissolved in milk. Mix well. Add lemon juice.

Pour mixture over apple slices in tin. Bake for 60–75 minutes.

Turn cake onto plate with apples as the topping. Carefully remove
baking paper.

Ginger Almond Cake

1 egg
175 g butter, melted
230 g plain flour
¼ teaspoon salt
210 g sugar
125 g glacé ginger, chopped
50 g whole blanched almonds
sugar, for sprinkling

Preheat the oven to 180°C. Lightly grease and flour a 20-cm round tin.

Beat the egg and, reserving a little to glaze the top, add to butter. Add sifted flour and salt, sugar and ginger pieces, and mix well.

Pour into prepared tin. Place almonds on top, brush with remainder of beaten egg and sprinkle with sugar. Bake for 45 minutes.

Gingerbread & Rhubarb Pudding

110 g softened butter

110 g brown sugar

2 eggs, lightly beaten

155 ml treacle

1 teaspoon ground ginger

1½ cups plain flour

1 level teaspoon bicarbonate of soda

⅓ cup milk

450 g rhubarb, trimmed and cut into small chunks

icing sugar, for dusting

Preheat the oven to 180°C. Grease a 1.5-litre ovenproof dish.

Cream the butter and sugar until light and fluffy. Slowly add the eggs. Pour in the treacle and mix well. Sift the ginger and the flour and stir into the batter. Dissolve the bicarbonate of soda in the milk and stir in. Spoon one-third of the mixture into the prepared dish and sprinkle with rhubarb. Spoon the rest of the batter over the top.

Bake for 45 minutes. Reduce the oven temperature to 160°C. Loosely cover the top of the pudding with foil and bake for a further 30 minutes.

Dust with icing sugar before serving with ice-cream or whipped cream.

SERVES 6–8

Gingerbread Ring

⅓ cup treacle

¾ cup brown sugar

125 g butter

1⅓ cups plain flour

2 teaspoons ground ginger

1½ teaspoons ground cinnamon

½ cup milk

1 teaspoon bicarbonate of soda

1 large egg, beaten

icing sugar, for dusting

Preheat the oven to 140°C. Lightly grease and flour a 22-cm ring cake tin.

Heat treacle, sugar and butter together, but do not boil. Add to sifted flour and spices. Warm milk in small saucepan and add bicarbonate of soda. Add to mixture with beaten egg.

Pour into prepared tin and bake for 75 minutes. Dust with icing sugar.

Like all gingerbread, this cake should be stored for a little while before eating to allow the flavour to mature.

Ginger & Sour Cream Cake

1½ cups self-raising flour

1½ teaspoons ground ginger

1½ cups brown sugar

3 eggs, lightly beaten

180 g butter, melted

½ cup sour cream

Preheat the oven to 180°C. Lightly grease a 23-cm round springform cake tin and line the base with non-stick baking paper.

Sift the flour and ginger into a mixing bowl and stir in the sugar. Stir in the eggs and melted butter. Combine to a smooth batter.

Spoon into the prepared tin and smear the sour cream over the top.

Bake for 45 minutes or until lightly browned on top.

Cool for 10 minutes in the tin on a rack. Turn out onto the rack and cool completely before serving.

Greek Hazelnut & Yoghurt Cake

3 large eggs, separated

⅔ cup brown sugar

3 tablespoons Greek-style yoghurt

grated zest of 1 lemon

160 g ground roasted hazelnuts

Preheat the oven to 180°C. Lightly grease a 16.5-cm × 22-cm oval tin or a 23-cm round springform cake tin and line the base with non-stick baking paper.

Whisk the egg yolks with the sugar until thick and creamy. Stir in the yoghurt, lemon zest and ground hazelnuts.

In another bowl, whip the egg whites until stiff. Carefully fold the whipped egg whites through the hazelnut mixture.

Spoon into the prepared tin and bake for 35 minutes or until cooked through.

Cool in the tin on a rack. Turn out onto a plate.

Serve with fresh fruit slices.

Hazelnut, Ricotta & Chocolate Cake

225 g softened butter

250 g castor sugar

6 eggs, separated

4 tablespoons plain flour

½ cup grated dark cooking chocolate

350 g ground roasted hazelnuts

400 g ricotta cheese

1 teaspoon vanilla extract

Preheat the oven to 160°C. Lightly grease a 23-cm round cake tin and line the base with non-stick baking paper.

Cream the butter and sugar until light and fluffy. Add the egg yolks one at a time.

Combine the sifted flour, chocolate and ground hazelnuts and fold into the batter. Stir in the ricotta and vanilla extract. Whisk the egg whites until soft peaks form and then fold into the batter.

Bake for 45–50 minutes or until the cake is cooked through. Cool in the tin before turning out.

Honey Cake

1 cup honey

2 cups warm water

2 cups sugar

4 cups flour

1 teaspoon baking powder

2 teaspoons ground cinnamon

1 teaspoon ground nutmeg

1 teaspoon ground ginger

1 teaspoon mace

½ teaspoon ground cloves

icing sugar, for dusting

Preheat the oven to 180°C. Lightly grease and flour a 20-cm cake tin.

Mix honey and warm water, then add to sugar and sifted dry ingredients, blending well.

Pour into prepared tin and bake for 50–60 minutes.

Dust with icing sugar.

Individual Baked Alaskas

BASE

125 g butter

90 g dark cooking chocolate, chopped

2 eggs

⅔ cup sugar

¾ cup chopped pecan nuts

1 cup plain flour

¼ cup milk

MERINGUE

2 egg whites

¼ teaspoon cream of tartar

¼ cup castor sugar

4 large scoops of chocolate ice-cream

Preheat the oven to 180°C. Lightly grease a 30-cm × 20-cm shallow baking dish and line with non-stick baking paper.

Melt the butter and chocolate in a saucepan over low heat, stirring occasionally. Remove from heat and cool a little.

Using an electric mixer, whisk the eggs and sugar together until pale and thick. Combine the nuts and sifted flour and add to the egg mixture, along with the melted chocolate and butter. Stir to combine and then stir in the milk.

Pour into the prepared dish and bake for 25–30 minutes, or until cooked through. Cool in the tin for 15 minutes and then place on a rack. ＞

To make the meringue mixture, place the 2 egg whites in a bowl with the cream of tartar and whisk with an electric beater until soft peaks form. Add in the castor sugar one spoonful at a time until the meringue mixture is shiny.

Preheat the oven to 220°C.

Scoop four large scoops of chocolate ice-cream onto a small baking tray and place in the freezer until ready to use.

Cut four even-sized pieces of brownie base to fit under the ice-cream scoops and place onto non-stick baking paper on a baking tray. (Cut the remaining brownie base into small squares and store for future use.)

Remove the ice-cream from the freezer and place on top of the brownie base. Using a spatula, spread the meringue carefully all over the ice-cream and brownie, making sure there is no ice-cream or base showing.

Bake for 3–4 minutes or until the meringue is lightly browned. Serve immediately.

SERVES 4

Individual Bread Puddings

6 slices of day-old white bread, torn into small pieces

300 ml milk

1 large apple, peeled, cored and grated

1 cup mixed dried fruit, finely chopped (pears, apples, sultanas, raisins)

80 g mixed peel

2 tablespoons brown sugar

2 tablespoons dark orange marmalade

60 g self-raising flour

2 eggs, beaten

1 teaspoon lemon juice

1 teaspoon ground cinnamon

1 teaspoon mixed spice

3 tablespoons butter, melted

icing sugar, for dusting

Preheat the oven to 150°C. Lightly grease six ramekin dishes.

Combine the bread and milk and leave to soak until soft (about 20 minutes). Beat well with a fork to form a smooth puree. Add the apple, mixed dried fruit and peel. Stir in the sugar, marmalade, sifted flour, eggs, lemon juice and spices. Add half of the melted butter and stir well.

Spoon the pudding into the six ramekin dishes and drizzle the remaining butter over the top. Bake for 45–60 minutes or until lightly browned and firm to the touch. Cool a little. Dust with icing sugar and serve with Pouring Custard (see page 215).

SERVES 6

Italian Polenta, Raisin & Ricotta Cake

150 g raisins

3 tablespoons brandy

200 g coarse polenta

1⅓ cups self-raising flour

1 heaped teaspoon baking
powder

250 g castor sugar

1 cup ricotta cheese

100 g butter, melted

175 ml warm water

Preheat the oven to 170°C. Lightly grease a 20-cm × 10-cm cake
tin and line the base with non-stick baking paper.

Place the raisins in a saucepan with the brandy and heat gently for
3–4 minutes until plumped up. Set aside to cool.

Combine the polenta, sifted flour and baking powder. Stir in the sugar,
ricotta, melted butter and water. Beat, using an electric mixer, until well
combined. Stir in the raisins and brandy.

Spoon the mixture into the prepared tin. Bake for 60–90 minutes or
until cooked through.

Cool in the tin for 20 minutes. Remove from the tin and cool on a rack.

Serve with whipped cream or mascarpone.

Italian Rice Tart

PASTRY

1⅓ cups plain flour

75 g chilled butter, cut into
    small pieces

1 egg, lightly beaten with 2
    tablespoons chilled water

FILLING

1 litre milk

180 g castor sugar

1 teaspoon vanilla extract

½ cup short-grain rice

grated zest of 1 lemon

30 g pine nuts

20 g currants

50 g fresh or frozen
    blackberries

icing sugar, for dusting

Preheat the oven to 180°C. Lightly grease a 23-cm flan dish.

Sift the flour into a food processor, add the chilled butter and blend until the mixture resembles fine breadcrumbs. Pour in the egg and water and process until just combined. Add more chilled water if necessary. Remove and knead lightly.

Roll out the pastry and use it to line the prepared dish. Chill in the fridge while you make the rice filling.

In a saucepan, bring the milk to the boil with the sugar and vanilla extract. Add the rice and cook for 20 minutes at a simmer. Remove and pour into a mixing bowl. Stir in the lemon zest, pine nuts, currants and blackberries. Leave to cool.

Pour into the prepared dish and bake for 30 minutes or until set and lightly browned on top. Cool completely before cutting.

Dust the top with icing sugar and serve with a puree of strawberries or raspberries.

Jolly Cake

175 g butter
175 g brown sugar
grated zest of 1 lemon
3 eggs, beaten
175 g self-raising flour
⅓ cup whisky

50 g butter
175 g icing sugar
1 tablespoon lemon juice
2 tablespoons thick honey

Preheat the oven to 190°C. Lightly grease two 18-cm sandwich tins and line the bases with non-stick baking paper.

Cream butter, sugar and lemon zest. Gradually beat in eggs, keeping mixture stiff. Fold in half the sifted flour, then the whisky and lastly the remaining flour.

Spoon into the two prepared tins. Bake for 20–25 minutes. Allow to cool on a rack.

To make lemon butter cream filling, beat together all ingredients. Sandwich cake together with half the butter cream and swirl the rest over the top.

Khaki Cake

1 cup milk

1 tablespoon golden syrup

½ teaspoon bicarbonate of soda

125 g butter

¾ cup sugar

1 egg

1½ cups plain flour

pinch of salt

1 teaspoon baking powder

1 tablespoon cocoa

⅓ cup sultanas or currants

1 teaspoon vanilla extract

desiccated coconut, for
decorating

Preheat the oven to 180°C. Lightly grease and flour a 23-cm ring tin.

Warm milk and golden syrup together. Add bicarbonate of soda and allow to cool. Cream butter and sugar, add egg and beat well. Sift flour, salt and baking powder and add to creamed mixture with cooled milk mixture. Beat well.

Pour half the mixture into the prepared tin. To remainder of mixture add cocoa, sultanas and vanilla extract. Pour on top. Bake for 45–60 minutes.

Ice with Chocolate Icing (see page 213) and sprinkle with coconut.

Lemon Delicious Pudding

3 tablespoons unsalted butter

85 g castor sugar

85 g self-raising flour

grated zest of 2 lemons

juice of 1 lemon

2 eggs, separated

300 ml milk

Preheat the oven to 180°C. Lightly grease a 1-litre ovenproof dish.

Cream the butter and sugar until light and fluffy. Sift in the flour, and add the lemon zest and juice. Whisk the egg yolks and milk and mix into the pudding batter until well combined. Whip the egg whites until stiff and carefully fold them into the pudding mixture.

Spoon the pudding mixture into the prepared dish and cook in a bain marie (see page xii). Bake for 30–35 minutes or until the sponge on top is golden.

Serve immediately.

SERVES 6

Lemon Meringue Pie

PASTRY

100 g chilled butter

1½ cups plain flour

1 teaspoon grated lemon zest

50 g icing sugar

1 egg, lightly beaten

2–3 tablespoons chilled water

FILLING

½ cup cornflour

1 cup castor sugar

½ cup lemon juice

1¼ cups water

3 egg yolks

3 tablespoons butter

MERINGUE

3 egg whites

½ cup castor sugar

Using a food processor, pulse the butter and flour until the mixture resembles fine breadcrumbs. Add the lemon zest and icing sugar and pulse for 1 minute.

Combine the egg and water and, with the motor running, slowly pour enough liquid into the food processor for the mixture to come together. Remove and roll into a ball. Chill for 30 minutes.

Preheat the oven to 220°C. Lightly grease a 24-cm flan dish. **>**

On a floured board, roll out the pastry to fit the flan dish. Blind-bake (see page xii) for 10–15 minutes or until lightly browned. Remove from the oven and reduce the oven temperature to 180°C.

To make filling, combine the cornflour and castor sugar in a saucepan and slowly stir in the lemon juice and water. Stir over a low heat until the mixture comes to the boil. Continue stirring until the mixture thickens. Remove from the heat and whisk in the egg yolks and butter. Cool, covered with baking paper, until ready to use.

To make meringue, whisk the egg whites until soft peaks form and then slowly add the castor sugar until the egg whites are stiff and glossy.

Spoon the filling onto the pastry shell and spread evenly. Spoon the meringue over the top. Bake on a preheated baking tray for 10–15 minutes or until the meringue is lightly browned.

Serve warm or cold with cream.

SERVES 8

Lemon Poppyseed Traybake

120 g softened butter

120 g castor sugar

175 g self-raising flour

1½ teaspoons baking powder

finely grated zest of 1 lemon

1 tablespoon poppy seeds

2 tablespoons milk

2 eggs, lightly beaten

100 g castor sugar, dissolved
in the juice of 1 lemon

Preheat the oven to 180°C. Lightly grease a 30-cm × 20-cm lamington pan and line with non-stick baking paper.

Cream the butter and sugar until light and fluffy. Sift the flour and baking powder together and fold into the butter mixture. Add the lemon zest, poppy seeds, milk and eggs. Mix to a smooth batter.

Pour into the prepared pan and smooth the top.

Bake for 20–25 minutes or until the cake is golden brown and pulls away from the sides of the pan. Brush the lemon syrup over the warm cake.

Allow to cool a little and then turn out onto a rack to cool completely. Cut into squares.

Lemon Seed Cake

1⅓ cups plain flour

3 tablespoons cornflour

¼ teaspoon baking powder

175 g butter

175 g castor sugar

grated zest of ½ lemon

3 eggs, lightly whisked

1 tablespoon hot water

2 teaspoons caraway seeds

Preheat the oven to 160°C. Lightly grease and flour a traditional bundt tin.

Sift flour, cornflour and baking powder. Cream butter and sugar, stir in grated lemon zest. Beat in eggs, adding a little sifted flour mixture to prevent curdling. Fold in remaining flour. Pour hot water over caraway seeds and add to cake mixture.

Pour into prepared tin and bake for 50 minutes, or until well risen and golden.

Lemon Semolina Cake
with Orange Glaze

¾ cup self-raising flour

1 teaspoon baking powder

1½ cups semolina

1 cup castor sugar

¾ cup yoghurt

½ cup buttermilk

½ cup canola oil

3 eggs

grated zest and juice of 1 lemon

GLAZE

½ cup orange marmalade

⅓ cup orange juice

candied citrus rind, for
decorating

Preheat the oven to 170°C. Lightly grease a 15-cm round deep cake
tin and line the base with non-stick baking paper.

Sift the flour, baking powder, semolina and sugar into a mixing bowl.
In another bowl, combine the yoghurt, buttermilk, oil, eggs, and lemon
zest and juice. Make a well in the centre and pour the wet mixture into
the dry ingredients. Stir to make a runny batter.

Pour into the prepared tin and bake for 55–70 minutes or until lightly
browned on top and cooked through. Cool in the tin for 5 minutes before
turning out onto a rack.

To make orange glaze, heat the marmalade and orange juice in a saucepan
and stir until melted. Pour over the cooled cake and allow to set. Decorate
with candied citrus rind. Serve with yoghurt mixed with a little honey.

Lemony Swiss Roll

LEMON CURD

finely grated zest and juice of
2 lemons

⅓ cup castor sugar

1 tablespoon cornflour

4 egg yolks

CAKE

4 large eggs, separated

⅔ cup castor sugar

125 ml lemon juice

grated zest of 2 lemons

50 g ground almonds

icing sugar, for dusting

FILLING

125 ml cream

4 tablespoons lemon curd
(above)

2 tablespoons toasted flaked
almonds

To make lemon curd, combine the lemon juice, sugar and cornflour
in a saucepan. Slowly bring to the boil and stir until mixture thickens.
Remove from the heat and whisk in the egg yolks and lemon zest.
Return to a gentle heat and cook for 2–3 minutes. Remove and allow
to cool. (Makes about 1 cup.)

Preheat the oven to 190°C. Lightly grease a 30-cm × 25-cm Swiss
roll tin and line with non-stick baking paper.

To make cake mixture, whisk the egg yolks and sugar until thick and creamy. Stir in the lemon juice and zest and the ground almonds. In another bowl, whip the egg whites until stiff. Carefully fold into the cake batter. Pour into the prepared tin.

Bake for 20–25 minutes or until set and lightly browned. Cool in the tin for 5–8 minutes. Carefully turn the cake out onto a double thickness of greaseproof paper and remove the baking paper. Cover with a tea towel until cool.

To make the filling, whip the cream until thick and fold in the lemon curd and flaked almonds. Spread over the cake and roll up carefully. Place on a serving platter, 'seam' side down, and dust liberally with icing sugar.

Lemony Treacle Tart

150 g chilled butter

2 cups plain flour

1 teaspoon grated lemon zest

50 g icing sugar

1 egg, lightly beaten

2–3 tablespoons chilled water

2 cups fresh breadcrumbs

3 eggs, lightly beaten

finely grated zest and juice
  of 1 lemon

350 ml golden syrup

150 ml cream

150 ml milk

Using a food processor, pulse the butter and flour until the mixture resembles fine breadcrumbs. Add the lemon zest and icing sugar and pulse for 1 minute.

Combine the egg and water and, with the motor running, slowly pour liquid into the food processor until the mixture comes together. Remove and roll into a ball. Chill for 30 minutes.

Preheat the oven to 180°C. Lightly grease a deep 23-cm loose-based tart tin.

On a floured board, roll out the pastry to fit the tart tin. Trim any excess pastry. Blind-bake (see page xii) for 10–15 minutes or until lightly golden. Remove from the oven. Reduce oven temperature to 170°C. **>**

Sprinkle the breadcrumbs over the prepared pastry shell. Combine all the filling ingredients in a food processor and blend until smooth. Pour into the tart tin and bake for 35 minutes or until the filling is golden and puffed up.

Cool in the tin before turning out and serving.

SERVES 8

Little Chocolate
Self-saucing Puddings

110 g dark cooking chocolate,
  chopped

115 g butter

4 eggs

130 g castor sugar

60 g plain flour

3 tablespoons ground almonds

Preheat the oven to 160°C. Lightly grease eight 125-ml ramekin dishes
or pudding bowls.

Melt the chocolate and butter in a small saucepan over a gentle heat.
Leave to cool.

Using an electric mixer, beat the eggs and sugar until pale and thick
(3–4 minutes). Combine the sifted flour and ground almonds and carefully
fold into the egg mixture.

Gently fold through the chocolate mixture. Spoon into the prepared
bowls and bake for 15–20 minutes or until just cooked but still a little
soft in the middle.

Serve warm, turned out onto individual plates, with Pouring Custard
(see page 215) or pureed raspberries.

SERVES 8

Little Christmas Cakes

875 g sultanas

375 g raisins

125 g currants

125 g mixed peel

200 g glacé cherries

¾ cup sherry

1 tablespoon orange marmalade

375 g softened butter

1½ cups brown sugar

6 eggs

3 cups plain flour

3 teaspoons mixed spice

Mix the fruit together with the sherry and marmalade and leave to soak overnight.

Preheat the oven to 145°C. Lightly grease and line four deep 12-cm square cake tins with a double thickness of non-stick baking paper.

Cream the butter and sugar until light and fluffy. Add the eggs one at a time until well combined. Sift the flour and mixed spice together and stir into the marinated fruit. Fold the butter mixture and fruit mixture together until well combined. Spoon the mixture evenly into the cake tins, smooth the top and push the mixture into the corners evenly. Bake for 2 hours (rotating the cakes every 30 minutes). Cool in the tins for 30 minutes before turning out onto a rack to cool completely.

Tie festive ribbon around the cakes, making a large, attractive bow on the top. Store in an airtight container until ready to eat or give away as Christmas presents.

Little Orange Sponge Puddings with Rhubarb Sauce

castor sugar, for coating

2 tablespoons butter

¾ cup castor sugar

grated zest of 2 oranges

¼ teaspoon salt

3 large eggs, separated

½ cup orange juice

½ cup milk

3 tablespoons plain flour

SAUCE

4 stalks rhubarb, trimmed
  and cut into small chunks

¼ cup brown sugar

2 tablespoons orange juice

Preheat the oven to 180°C. Lightly grease six 125-ml ramekin dishes or tea cups and sprinkle a little castor sugar inside to coat the sides and base.

Cream the butter and a third of the sugar until light and fluffy. Add the orange zest, salt and egg yolks and beat well. Mix in the orange juice, milk and sifted flour. In another bowl, whisk the egg whites until soft peaks form and then slowly whisk in remaining sugar.

Gently fold the egg whites into the egg-yolk mixture. Spoon into the prepared dishes and place in a bain marie (see page xii). Bake for 35 minutes or until puffed up. Place puddings on a rack to cool. Turn them out onto individual plates and serve with a spoonful of rhubarb sauce.

To make the sauce, cook the rhubarb with the sugar and orange juice in a saucepan over a gentle heat for 8–10 minutes. Cool to room temperature.

SERVES 6

Little Sticky Date Puddings
with Hot Butterscotch Sauce

1¼ cups chopped stoned dates

1¼ cups water

1 teaspoon bicarbonate of soda

3 tablespoons softened butter

¾ cup castor sugar

2 eggs, lightly beaten

1 cup self-raising flour

SAUCE

½ cup cream

100 g butter

½ cup brown sugar

Preheat the oven to 180°C. Lightly grease a six-cup jumbo muffin tin.

Place the dates and water in a saucepan and bring to the boil, simmering for about 5 minutes or until the dates are softened. Remove from the heat and stir in the bicarbonate of soda.

Cream the butter and sugar until light and fluffy. Add the eggs a little at a time, beating after each addition to make a smooth batter. Fold in the sifted flour and then stir in the date-and-water mixture until well combined.

Spoon into the prepared muffin cups and bake for 20 minutes or until firm and springy to touch.

To make the butterscotch sauce, combine all the ingredients in a saucepan and stir over a low heat until the butter is melted. Simmer for 10 minutes or until thickened.

Turn the puddings out and serve warm on individual plates with hot butterscotch sauce poured over the top.

Madeira Cake

175 g softened butter

175 g castor sugar

grated zest of 1 lemon

1½ cups plain flour

1 teaspoon baking powder

3 eggs, lightly beaten

2 tablespoons milk

3 slices candied citrus peel,
   cut into small pieces

Preheat the oven to 180°C. Lightly grease a 20-cm × 10-cm loaf tin and line the base with non-stick baking paper.

Cream the butter, sugar and lemon zest until light and fluffy. Sift flour with baking powder. Slowly add the eggs, alternating with a tablespoon of flour. Fold in remaining flour and then the milk.

Pour into the prepared tin and bake for 60 minutes. Sprinkle with the citrus peel and return to the oven. Bake for a further 30 minutes or until lightly browned, risen and cooked through. Cool in the tin for 15 minutes before carefully turning out onto a rack to cool completely.

Marble Cake

50 g dark cooking chocolate, chopped

175 g softened butter

175 g castor sugar

3 eggs, lightly beaten

⅓ cup milk

175 g self-raising flour

½ teaspoon baking powder

Preheat the oven to 180°C. Lightly grease a 20-cm round cake tin and line the base with non-stick baking paper.

Melt chocolate in a bowl over hot water, and keep warm. Cream the butter and sugar until soft and fluffy. Add the eggs a little at a time until well combined. Add milk and stir until combined. Stir in the sifted flour and baking powder. Remove half of the mixture and stir in the melted chocolate until well combined.

Drop spoonfuls of the cake mixtures into the prepared tin, alternating between mixtures and starting with the light mixture. Bake for 60–75 minutes or until cooked through.

Cool in the tin for 10 minutes before turning out onto a rack to cool completely.

Mary's Chocolate Cake

250 g softened butter

3 cups plain flour

2 cups castor sugar

¾ cup cocoa

2 teaspoons bicarbonate of soda

1 teaspoon salt

2 cups milk

3 eggs

1 tablespoon vinegar

1½ teaspoons vanilla extract

1 tablespoon coffee liqueur, optional

Preheat the oven to 180°C. Lightly grease and line two 20-cm round cake tins or grease and flour a traditional bundt tin.

To butter add sifted dry ingredients and milk, then beat for 2 minutes with an electric mixer. Add eggs, vinegar, vanilla and coffee liqueur and beat well.

Pour into prepared tin. Bake for 45–60 minutes, depending on the size of the tin/s used.

Ice cakes with Chocolate Icing (see page 213). Or cut cakes in half or layers, sprinkle with coffee liqueur, fill with whipped cream and dust with icing sugar.

Makes two large cakes or a bundt.

May's Date Cake

1 cup chopped stoned dates

1 teaspoon bicarbonate of soda

1 cup boiling water

125 g butter

½ cup sugar

pinch of salt

¼ teaspoon vanilla extract

2 eggs

1 teaspoon grated lemon
    or orange zest

¾ cup desiccated coconut

1¾ cups plain flour

1 teaspoon baking powder

icing sugar, for dusting

Preheat the oven to 180°C. Lightly grease and flour a 20-cm cake tin.

Combine dates, bicarbonate of soda and boiling water. Leave for
20 minutes then beat to a pulp. Cream butter, sugar, salt and vanilla
extract. Add eggs one at a time, beating well after each addition. Fold
in date pulp, zest and coconut, then add sifted flour and baking powder.

Pour into prepared tin and bake for 40–45 minutes.

Dust with icing sugar or ice as required.

This cake keeps well.

Moll's Fruit Cake

1 × 225-g tin crushed pineapple,
  undrained

225 g butter

¾ cup brown sugar

725 g mixed dried fruit

3 eggs, beaten

1 cup self-raising flour

1 cup plain flour

½ teaspoon bicarbonate
  of soda

1 teaspoon baking powder

1 teaspoon almond extract

1 teaspoon lemon essence

1 teaspoon ground cloves

2 teaspoons mixed spice

Preheat the oven to 140°C. Lightly grease a 23-cm cake tin and line with two layers of non-stick baking paper.

Bring pineapple, butter, sugar and mixed fruit to the boil. Take off heat. When cool, add remaining ingredients and mix.

Pour into prepared tin and bake for 90 minutes, or until cooked. Leave to cool in tin before turning out.

Moroccan Date & Walnut Cake

150 g butter

125 g sugar

4 eggs

1 cup self-raising flour

1 teaspoon ground cinnamon

1 teaspoon ground nutmeg

½ teaspoon ground cloves

½ cup milk

½ teaspoon vanilla extract

1 cup chopped stoned dates

½ cup chopped walnuts

2 tablespoons plain flour

Preheat the oven to 160°C. Lightly grease a 20-cm square cake tin and line the base with non-stick baking paper.

Cream the butter and sugar until light and fluffy. Add the eggs one at a time. Sift the self-raising flour and spices together and stir into the egg mixture, combining well. Stir in the milk and vanilla extract. Mix the dates and walnuts with the flour and fold through the cake batter.

Spoon into the prepared tin and bake for 30–60 minutes or until cooked through.

Cool in the tin for 5 minutes before turning out onto a rack.

Serve with fresh cream and orange segments.

Nola's Plum Duff

225 g raisins

225 g sultanas

225 g currants

175 g mixed peel

2¾ cups suet

200 g sugar

2⅓ cups plain flour

2 teaspoons mixed spice

2 teaspoons ground cinnamon

¼ teaspoon ground nutmeg

2 teaspoons baking powder

pinch of salt

3 eggs, beaten

1 cup milk

In a large bowl combine fruit, suet, sugar and sifted dry ingredients. Add beaten eggs and milk and stir well.

Spoon into two or three greased pudding basins and steam for 2½–3 hours.

Alternatively, this pudding may be cooked in a pudding cloth. Scald a square of calico in boiling water, wring and dust with flour while still warm. Place mixture in centre and gather up ends, shaping mixture into ball, then tie tightly with string. Put into boiling water with a plate on the bottom of pan. If making as one pudding, boil 4½ hours, topping up water as needed. Hang to dry before storing.

To serve, boil 60 minutes.

This pudding will keep for many months. Serve with brandy sauce.

Nutty Orange & Lemon Cake

3 eggs, separated

¾ cup castor sugar

grated zest of 1 lemon

grated zest of 1 small orange

1 teaspoon vanilla extract

½ cup finely ground hazelnuts

½ cup finely ground almonds

½ cup self-raising flour

pinch of salt

Preheat the oven to 170°C. Lightly grease a 23-cm round cake tin and line the base with non-stick baking paper.

Whisk the egg yolks and sugar until thick and creamy (about 3 minutes). Stir in the lemon and orange zest and vanilla extract. Mix the ground nuts together with the flour and fold into the egg mixture. In another bowl, whip the egg whites with a pinch of salt until stiff. Carefully fold two large spoonfuls of egg whites through the nutty cake batter. Tip the cake batter into the egg whites and carefully fold through.

Spoon into the prepared tin and bake for 25–30 minutes or until lightly browned and cooked through. Cool in the tin for 10 minutes before turning out onto a rack.

Serve warm or cold with fresh berries and whipped cream.

Old-fashioned Gingerbread

225 g softened butter

1 cup castor sugar

3 eggs, lightly beaten

1 cup treacle

1 cup milk

3 cups plain flour

1 teaspoon ground cinnamon

1 teaspoon grated nutmeg

2 teaspoons ground ginger

2 teaspoons bicarbonate of soda

Preheat the oven to 160°C. Lightly grease a 23-cm square cake tin and line the base with non-stick baking paper.

Cream the butter and sugar until light and fluffy. Slowly add the eggs until well combined. Heat the treacle and milk in a saucepan. Remove and cool a little before stirring into the egg-and-butter mixture. Sift the flour, spices and bicarbonate of soda together. Fold into the wet ingredients.

Spoon the cake batter into the prepared tin and bake for 60 minutes or until cooked through.

Cool in the tin before turning the cake out onto a rack to cool completely.

Old French Fig Cake

225 g fresh ripe figs, chopped
   finely or minced

125 g butter

2 cups sugar

1 egg, lightly beaten

3⅔ cups plain flour

2 teaspoons baking powder

¼ teaspoon salt

½ tablespoon grated lemon
   or orange zest

½ teaspoon vanilla extract

icing sugar, for dusting

Preheat the oven to 150°C. Lightly grease a 20-cm cake tin and line the base with non-stick baking paper.

Place figs in saucepan and simmer for 8 minutes. Add butter and sugar and keep stirring over gentle heat until melted. Allow to cool.

Stir egg into mixture. Add sifted flour, baking powder, salt, zest and vanilla extract.

Pour into prepared tin and bake for 60–90 minutes.

Dust with icing sugar.

Orange Cake

1 cup plain flour

¾ cup sugar

3 tablespoons milk

3 eggs, beaten

75 g butter, melted

grated zest of ½ orange

1½ teaspoons baking powder

Preheat the oven to 180°C. Lightly grease and flour an 18-cm cake tin.

Sift flour and mix all ingredients together except baking powder. Leave for a few minutes. Beat for 3 minutes then add baking powder.

Pour into prepared tin and bake for 30 minutes. Ice with Orange Icing (see page 215).

Orange-iced Chocolate Teacake

100 g softened butter

⅔ cup castor sugar

2 large eggs, lightly beaten

2 tablespoons cocoa dissolved in
    2 tablespoons hot water

grated zest of 1 orange

⅔ cup self-raising flour

2 tablespoons freshly
    squeezed orange juice

3 slices glacé orange, for
    decorating

Preheat the oven to 180°C. Lightly grease a 20-cm round cake tin
and line the base with non-stick baking paper.

Cream the butter and sugar until light and fluffy. Slowly add the eggs
until combined. Beat in the cocoa mixture and orange zest. Fold in the
sifted flour and mix in the orange juice.

Spoon the batter into the prepared tin and bake for 40–45 minutes or
until cooked through. Cool in the tin for 10–15 minutes before turning
out onto a rack.

When cold, spread Orange Icing (see page 215) over the sides and top
of the cake using a spatula. Decorate with chopped glacé orange slices.

Passionfruit Cake

50 g softened butter

125 g sugar

2 eggs

1 tablespoon passionfruit juice

1 tablespoon water

½ cup plain flour

1 teaspoon baking powder

1½ tablespoons cornflour

FILLING

1 tablespoon gelatine powder

2 tablespoons water

1 cup cream

5–6 passionfruit

sugar, to sweeten

icing sugar, for dusting

Preheat the oven to 180°C. Lightly grease and flour two 15-cm round deep cake tins.

Cream butter and sugar. Beat eggs well, then add passionfruit juice and water. Sift dry ingredients and add alternately with egg mixture to creamed mixture.

Pour into prepared tins and bake for about 15 minutes. Turn onto a rack to cool.

To make passionfruit cream filling, dissolve gelatine powder in water over gentle heat. Whip cream stiffly, then add passionfruit and sugar. Stir in dissolved gelatine.

Join cake with passionfruit cream and dust with icing sugar.

Peanut Butterscotch Cake

TOPPING

125 g butter

2 tablespoons brown sugar

2 tablespoons white sugar

2 tablespoons honey

1½ cups finely chopped peanuts

CAKE

1⅔ cups plain flour

½ teaspoon salt

3 teaspoons baking powder

125 g butter

½ cup sugar

2 eggs, beaten

¼ cup milk

½ teaspoon vanilla extract

Lightly grease a 23-cm square tin and line base with non-stick baking paper.

To make nut topping, melt butter, sugars and honey in saucepan. Stir in peanuts. Pour nut mixture into prepared tin.

Preheat the oven to 190°C.

To make cake, sift flour, salt and baking powder. Rub in butter, add sugar and mix. Pour eggs into centre, add milk and vanilla extract, and mix well.

Pour cake mixture on top of nut mixture. Bake for 40 minutes, then reduce heat to 180°C and bake for a further 20 minutes. Turn out immediately onto a rack and remove paper. Replace any nut topping that comes away – it will set in position as it cools.

Pear, Chocolate & Almond Traybake

125 g butter

200 g dark cooking chocolate, chopped

3 eggs

1 cup castor sugar

1 cup self-raising flour

1 cup ground almonds

2 large Beurre Bosc pears, peeled,
   cored and thinly sliced

Preheat the oven to 180°C. Lightly grease a 28-cm × 18-cm lamington pan and line with non-stick baking paper.

Melt the butter in a saucepan over a medium heat. Remove and stir in the chocolate until melted.

Beat the eggs and sugar until pale and thick. Slowly pour in the chocolate mixture and stir gently to combine. Carefully fold in the sifted flour and ground almonds. Pour the batter into the prepared pan. Arrange the pear slices over the top of the batter.

Bake for 40–45 minutes or until firm and cooked through.

Cool on a rack. Cut into slices and serve with Pouring Custard (see page 215) or cream.

Pear & Prune Cake

100 g softened butter

250 g castor sugar

3 large eggs

220 g plain flour

1 teaspoon ground cinnamon

1 teaspoon baking powder

⅓ cup milk

1 tablespoon brandy

2 firm ripe pears, peeled, cored and cut into small chunks

100 g stoned prunes, roughly chopped

2 tablespoons castor sugar

Preheat the oven to 180°C. Lightly grease a 20-cm round springform cake tin and line the base with non-stick baking paper.

Cream the butter and sugar until light and fluffy. Add the eggs one at a time until well combined. Sift the flour, cinnamon and baking powder into another bowl. Spoon the flour mixture into the butter mixture, alternating with the milk to form a smooth batter. Stir in the brandy. Fold the pears and prunes into the batter.

Pour into the prepared tin, sprinkle second measure of castor sugar over the top and bake for 45–55 minutes or until the cake is cooked through. Cool in the tin on a rack.

Turn out and serve with ice-cream or whipped cream.

Pear & Raisin Crumble

1.2 kg ripe pears, peeled, cored
and cut into small chunks

½ cup brown sugar

½ cup raisins

2 tablespoons plain flour, sifted

2 tablespoons sherry

1 tablespoon finely chopped
crystallised ginger

TOPPING

1 cup plain flour

1 cup walnuts, finely
chopped

⅔ cup brown sugar

120 g butter, cut into
tiny pieces

Preheat the oven to 190°C. Lightly grease six 150-ml ramekin dishes.

Combine all the fruit mixture ingredients and spoon into the prepared dish.

To make the topping, combine the flour, chopped walnuts, sugar and butter
until the mixture starts to clump together.

Spoon the topping over the fruit mixture and bake for 30 minutes or until
the topping is golden and crisp.

Cool a little before serving with plain yoghurt or Pouring Custard (see
page 215).

SERVES 8

Pineapple Blitztorte

110 g softened butter

85 g castor sugar

4 egg yolks

2 tablespoons milk

¾ cup plain flour

1 level teaspoon baking powder

MERINGUE

4 egg whites

140 g castor sugar

30 g flaked almonds

2 teaspoons castor sugar mixed
with ½ teaspoon ground
cinnamon

FILLING

1 cup cream, whipped with
1 teaspoon sugar until fluffy

200 g sweet fresh pineapple,
peeled, cored and finely
chopped

Preheat the oven to 175°C. Lightly butter and flour two 22-cm round cake tins and line the bases with non-stick baking paper.

Cream the butter and sugar until light and fluffy. Add the egg yolks and milk. Sift the flour and baking powder and stir into the batter. Spoon evenly into the prepared tins.

To make meringue, whip the egg whites until stiff and then whisk in sugar until thick and glossy.

Spread meringue over the cake batters. Scatter the flaked almonds over the top and sprinkle with cinnamon sugar.

Bake for 30 minutes or until the meringue is lightly browned. Cool in the tins before filling.

Turn one cake out onto a plate with the meringue side down. Spread the whipped cream over the cake and sprinkle with chopped pineapple. Place the other cake on top, with the meringue side up, and serve.

Pineapple & Carrot Cake

3 eggs, beaten

½ cup vegetable oil

1 cup brown sugar

1 cup sugar

2 teaspoons vanilla extract

2 cups wholemeal flour

2 teaspoons ground cinnamon

1 teaspoon ground nutmeg

½ teaspoon salt

2 teaspoons bicarbonate of soda

¼ cup sour cream

3 cups grated peeled carrot

1 cup desiccated coconut

1 × 225-g tin crushed pineapple, drained

Preheat the oven to 180°C. Lightly grease and flour a 22-cm ring tin.

Combine eggs, oil, sugars and vanilla extract, and mix well. Stir in sifted flour, spices, salt and bicarbonate of soda. Fold in sour cream, grated carrot, coconut and pineapple.

Pour into prepared tin and bake for 90 minutes, or until cooked. Ice with Cream Cheese Icing (see page 214).

Plum Kuchen

1½ cups plain flour

1½ teaspoons baking powder

1 teaspoon ground cinnamon

pinch of salt

100 g softened butter

⅔ cup castor sugar

2 large eggs

2 teaspoons vanilla extract

½ teaspoon almond extract

½ cup sour cream

5 large plums, each cut into 8 slices

¼ cup castor sugar mixed with ½ teaspoon ground cinnamon

2 tablespoons butter, melted

Preheat the oven to 175°C. Lightly grease a 2-litre ovenproof dish.

Sift the dry ingredients into a bowl. In another bowl, cream the butter and first measure of sugar until light and fluffy. Beat in the eggs one at a time, then stir in the vanilla and almond extract. Stir in the dry ingredients, alternating with the sour cream, to make a smooth batter. Spread into the prepared tin and arrange the plum slices in four rows on top.

Sprinkle cinnamon sugar over the plums. Drizzle with the melted butter.

Bake for 40 minutes or until firm and springy to the touch.

Cool for at least 30 minutes before cutting and serving.

Potato Caramel Cake

150 g butter

2 cups sugar

4 eggs, separated

½ cup milk

½ cup hot mashed potato

½ teaspoon salt

¾ teaspoon ground cloves

¾ teaspoon ground cinnamon

¾ teaspoon ground nutmeg

1 cup grated dark cooking
chocolate

2 teaspoons baking powder

2 cups plain flour

1 cup chopped walnuts

Preheat the oven to 180°C. Lightly grease and flour a 20-cm square cake tin.

Cream butter, sugar and egg yolks. Add milk, mashed potato, salt, spices and chocolate. Sift baking powder with flour and stir into batter. Fold in stiffly beaten egg whites. Add chopped walnuts just as cake is ready for the oven.

Pour into prepared tin and bake for 60–75 minutes, or until cooked. Ice with Chocolate Icing (see page 213).

Pumpkin Cake

250 g butter

2½ cups sugar

3 eggs

3 cups wholemeal flour

1 teaspoon bicarbonate of soda

1 teaspoon baking powder

1 teaspoon ground cinnamon

1 teaspoon allspice

½ teaspoon ground nutmeg

2 cups mashed pumpkin

1 cup chopped walnuts

walnuts and cinnamon for decorating

Preheat the oven to 125°C. Lightly grease and flour a 23-cm cake tin.

Cream butter and sugar. Add eggs one at a time, beating well after each addition. Sift dry ingredients, and add alternately with pumpkin to creamed mixture. Add chopped walnuts and beat well.

Pour into prepared tin and bake for 90 minutes, or until cooked. Ice with Lemon Icing (see page 214). Sprinkle with walnuts and cinnamon.

Pumpkin Fruit Cake

125 g sultanas

125 g raisins

125 g mixed peel

125 g dried apricots, finely chopped

1 cup orange or apple juice

1 tablespoon honey

1 teaspoon bicarbonate of soda

4 egg whites

1 cup cold mashed pumpkin

1¾ cups self-raising wholemeal flour

1 teaspoon mixed spice

Preheat the oven to 165°C. Lightly grease a 20-cm round cake tin and line the base with non-stick baking paper.

In a small saucepan combine fruit, juice and honey. (This cake is even more delicious if the dried fruit is soaked in the orange juice overnight – for a special occasion several teaspoons of brandy can be added.) Bring to boil, stirring gently. Remove from heat and add bicarbonate of soda. Allow to cool.

In a large bowl beat egg whites lightly, add fruit mixture and mashed pumpkin and beat until smooth. Stir in flour and mixed spice, combining well.

Pour into prepared tin and bake for 90 minutes or until cooked.

Raisin Orange Cake

125 g butter

1 cup sugar

1 teaspoon vanilla extract

2 eggs, beaten

1 medium-sized orange

1 cup raisins

½ cup chopped walnuts

2 cups plain flour

pinch of salt

½ cup warm water

1 teaspoon bicarbonate
of soda

Preheat the oven to 180°C. Lightly grease and flour a 15-cm round deep cake tin.

Cream butter, sugar and vanilla extract. Add eggs and mix well.

Cut washed, unpeeled orange into quarters. Remove peel, outer pith and seeds. Put flesh through mincer or blender with raisins and walnuts. Add to creamed mixture.

Fold in sifted flour and salt alternately with warm water in which bicarbonate of soda has been dissolved.

Pour into prepared tin and bake for 60–70 minutes. Ice with Orange Icing (see page 215).

Red Devil Cake

1 cup grated dark cooking
   chocolate

½ cup milk, mixed with
   ½ tablespoon lemon
   juice or vinegar

1 cup brown sugar

1 egg yolk

½ cup butter

1 cup brown sugar

3 egg yolks

1 teaspoon bicarbonate
   of soda

½ cup milk

2 cups plain flour

2 egg whites

Preheat the oven to 180°C. Lightly grease and flour a 20-cm round cake tin.

Simmer together chocolate, sour milk, first measure of brown sugar and one egg yolk until dissolved. Set aside to cool.

Cream butter and second measure of sugar, add remaining egg yolks, bicarbonate of soda dissolved in milk, and sifted flour. Beat egg whites until stiff and fold into mixture with chocolate mixture.

Pour into prepared tin and bake for 50–60 minutes. Ice with Chocolate Icing (see page 213).

This mixture can also be baked in sandwich tins and joined with chocolate icing. Halve the cooking time if using this method.

Rhubarb & Lemon Cake

1 cup castor sugar

finely grated zest of 2 lemons

4 eggs, lightly beaten

¼ cup milk

1¾ cups self-raising flour

1 tablespoon fresh lemon juice

140 g butter, melted

⅔ cup light olive oil

300 g fresh rhubarb, trimmed
and cut into small chunks

Preheat the oven to 180°C. Line a 26-cm round springform cake tin with non-stick baking paper, and lightly butter and flour the sides.

Using an electric mixer, blend the sugar with the lemon zest for 1 minute. Add the eggs and beat until pale and thick (about 3 minutes).

Stir in the milk and sifted flour to make a smooth batter. Blend in the lemon juice, melted butter and oil.

Pour one-third of the batter into the prepared tin, making sure the base is covered. Arrange the rhubarb over the top and then pour the remaining batter over the rhubarb.

Bake for 50 minutes or until the cake pulls away from the sides of the tin. Cool for 10 minutes before turning out onto a rack.

Rhubarb & Ricotta Crumble

CRUMBLE

150 g butter

1 cup plain flour

1 cup brown sugar

100 g rolled oats

FILLING

2 cups ricotta cheese

3 eggs

4 tablespoons castor sugar

2 tablespoons orange juice

400 g cooked rhubarb, pureed

Preheat the oven to 180°C. Lightly grease a 23-cm springform pan and line the base with non-stick baking paper.

To make crumble, combine the butter, flour, brown sugar and rolled oats in a food processor and pulse until the mixture starts to clump together. Reserve ¾ cup of the mixture, and press the rest into the prepared pan.

Bake for 15–20 minutes or until lightly browned and firm.

To make the filling, combine the ricotta, eggs, castor sugar and orange juice. Mix well until smooth.

Spread the pureed rhubarb over the baked crumble base. Pour in the ricotta mixture. Sprinkle the reserved crumble over, and bake for 35–40 minutes. Cool to room temperature.

SERVES 6

Rich Chocolate Cake

1¼ cups plain flour

1½ teaspoons baking powder

¾ teaspoon bicarbonate of soda

pinch of salt

100 g dark cooking chocolate, chopped

1½ cups castor sugar

½ cup boiling water

3 large eggs, lightly beaten

1 heaped tablespoon cocoa

225 g softened butter, cut into 8 pieces

¾ cup sour cream

1 tablespoon dark rum

Preheat the oven to 170°C. Lightly grease a 23-cm round springform cake tin and line the base with non-stick baking paper.

Blend the sifted flour, baking powder, bicarbonate of soda and salt in a food processor for 3 seconds. Remove and reserve.

Process the chocolate and half of the sugar until the mixture resembles fine breadcrumbs.

With the food processor running, pour in the boiling water and process until the chocolate has melted. Pour in the eggs, cocoa and remaining sugar. Process for 2 minutes. Add in the butter and process for 1 minute. Add the sour cream and rum. ➤

Spoon the flour into the food processor. Pulse the mixture three or four times until the flour is incorporated. Be careful not to over-process.

Spoon the mixture into the prepared tin. Bake for 75 minutes or until cooked through. Cool in the tin for 10 minutes before turning out onto a rack.

Rich Chocolate & Date Cake

250 g whole unblanched almonds

250 g dark cooking chocolate, chopped

250 g chopped stoned dates

6 large egg whites

pinch of salt

½ cup castor sugar

Preheat the oven to 180°C. Lightly grease a 23-cm round springform cake tin and line the base with non-stick baking paper.

Chop the nuts and chocolate together using a food processor. Transfer to a mixing bowl and stir in the chopped dates. In another bowl, whisk the egg whites and salt until soft peaks form. Slowly whisk in the sugar until thick and glossy. Fold the chocolate mixture through the meringue.

Pour into the prepared tin and bake for 45 minutes or until firm. Cool in the tin and then carefully turn out onto a platter.

Cut into thin wedges and serve with fresh fruit slices and cream.

Rich Old-fashioned Fruit Cake

1 kg mixed dried fruit

½ cup finely chopped glacé
   ginger

1 teaspoon grated orange zest

1 cup apple puree

2 tablespoons apricot jam

2 tablespoons orange juice

250 g butter

1¼ cups brown sugar

1 teaspoon vanilla extract

4 eggs, lightly beaten

3 cups plain flour

1 teaspoon baking powder

1 teaspoon mixed spice

1 teaspoon ground ginger

glacé cherries and whole
   almonds, for decorating

2–4 tablespoons whisky

In a large bowl mix fruit, glacé ginger, orange zest, apple puree, apricot jam and orange juice. Cover and allow to stand overnight.

Preheat the oven to 150°C. Lightly grease a 20-cm round tin and line with two layers of non-stick baking paper.

Cream butter, sugar and vanilla extract until light and creamy. Add eggs one at a time. Add sifted dried ingredients alternately with fruit mixture.

Put into prepared tin. Decorate with rows of cherries and almonds. Bake for 3–3½ hours. Cover with kitchen paper for the last hour to prevent burning.

Remove from oven and pour whisky on top. Leave in tin to cool completely before removing.

Roasted Pecan & Ginger Cake

130 g softened butter

1 cup brown sugar

2 eggs, lightly beaten

1 cup plain flour

½ tablespoon baking powder

2 teaspoons ground ginger

⅔ cup roasted pecans, finely chopped

⅔ cup milk

½ teaspoon freshly grated ginger

½ teaspoon vanilla extract

10 pecan halves, for decorating

Preheat the oven to 180°C. Lightly grease a 22-cm round cake tin and line the base with non-stick baking paper.

Cream the butter and sugar until light and fluffy. Slowly add the eggs. Sift the flour, baking powder and ground ginger into another bowl and stir in the pecans. Add the flour mixture to the butter mixture a little at a time, alternating with the milk and finishing with the flour mixture. Stir in the fresh ginger and vanilla extract.

Pour into the prepared tin and decorate the top with the pecan halves.

Bake for 35–40 minutes or until lightly browned and cooked through. Cool on a rack for 10 minutes before turning out of the tin to cool completely.

Rum & Lime Glazed Banana Bread

120 g softened butter

¾ cup brown sugar

2 eggs, lightly beaten

1 cup mashed banana

3 tablespoons buttermilk

1 tablespoon fresh lime juice

½ teaspoon salt

½ teaspoon ground ginger

2 cups self-raising flour

½ teaspoon bicarbonate
of soda

GLAZE

¼ cup brown sugar

1 tablespoon rum

1 tablespoon butter

3 tablespoons fresh lime juice

Preheat the oven to 175°C. Lightly grease a 25-cm × 15-cm loaf pan and line the base with non-stick baking paper.

Cream butter and sugar until light and fluffy. Stir in the eggs, mashed banana, buttermilk and lime juice and combine. Sift the salt, ginger and flour into a mixing bowl with the bicarbonate of soda. Stir into the cake batter and combine until smooth. Spoon into prepared pan and bake for 60 minutes. Allow cake to stand for 10 minutes before turning out onto a rack.

Meanwhile, heat all the glaze ingredients in a saucepan. Stir for about 5 minutes to form a smooth syrup.

Coat the top and sides of the cake with the glaze. Serve while warm or at room temperature.

Ruth's Sponge Cake

2 tablespoons chilled water

¾ cup sugar

4 eggs, separated

1½ cups cornflour

2 teaspoons plain flour (optional)

1 teaspoon baking powder

1 teaspoon vanilla extract

whipped cream and jam, for filling

icing sugar, for dusting

Preheat the oven to 190°C. Lightly grease and flour two 20-cm round cake tins.

Warm water and sugar in saucepan. Beat egg whites until stiff. Add sugar mixture and beat well. Add yolks one at a time, and beat until thick. Stir in sifted cornflour, flour and baking powder. Lastly add vanilla extract.

Pour into prepared tins and bake for 20–25 minutes. If you are brave enough, take the sponge straight from the oven and, still in the tin, drop it on the floor to get rid of excess air.

Fill with whipped cream and jam and dust with icing sugar.

Seed Cake

125 g softened butter

125 g castor sugar

2 eggs, beaten

125 g self-raising flour

½ teaspoon baking powder

50 g ground almonds

2 heaped teaspoons caraway seeds

3 tablespoons yoghurt

4 teaspoons toasted rolled oats

icing sugar, for dusting

Preheat the oven to 180°C. Lightly grease a 20-cm round cake tin and line the base with non-stick baking paper.

Cream the butter and sugar until light and fluffy. Slowly add the eggs until well combined. Sift the flour and baking powder into another bowl. Stir in the ground almonds and caraway seeds. Fold into the butter mixture and stir in the yoghurt.

Spoon into the prepared tin, sprinkle with oats and dust with icing sugar.

Bake for 45–60 minutes or until the cake is cooked through. Cool in the tin for 10 minutes before turning out onto a rack to cool completely.

Sesame Pound Cake

⅓ cup sesame seeds

110 g butter

1 cup sugar

4 eggs

2 cups plain flour

½ teaspoon salt

1 teaspoon baking powder

½ cup milk

1 teaspoon vanilla extract

1 teaspoon sesame oil

1 teaspoon grated lemon zest

Preheat the oven to 160°C. Lightly grease a 23-cm springform tin and line the base with non-stick baking paper.

Toast sesame seeds in frying pan for 2 minutes until golden. Cream butter and sugar. Add eggs one at a time, beating well after each addition. In another bowl sift flour, salt and baking powder, and stir in all but 1 tablespoon of sesame seeds.

In a large cup combine milk, vanilla extract, oil and lemon zest. To butter mixture add sifted dry ingredients alternately with milk mixture, stirring well. Do not beat or over-stir.

Pour into prepared tin, sprinkle with remaining sesame seeds and bake for 50–60 minutes, or until cooked.

Simple Tarte Tatin

⅔ cup brown sugar

½ teaspoon ground cardamom

100 g butter

6–8 Golden Delicious apples, peeled,
   cored and quartered lengthways

1 sheet frozen puff pastry, thawed

Preheat the oven to 220°C.

Sprinkle the sugar and cardamom over the bottom of a 24-cm ovenproof
frying pan or skillet and dot with the butter.

Tightly pack the apple quarters into the pan, with the rounded sides
pressed down into the sugar.

Cook over a high heat until the sugar and butter caramelises the apples.
Remove from the heat and place the puff pastry on top, trimming the
edges a little.

Place the frying pan on a preheated oven tray and bake for 10–15 minutes
or until the pastry is cooked. Remove from the oven and cool a little.
Carefully invert the tart onto a plate and serve with Pouring Custard (see
page 215) or cream.

SERVES 6

Sour Cream Poppy Seed Cake

½ cup butter

½ cup poppy seeds

1 cup honey

1 teaspoon vanilla extract

4 eggs

1½ cups plain flour

1 teaspoon bicarbonate of soda

¼ teaspoon salt

½ cup wholemeal flour

1 cup sour cream

TOPPING

250 g cream cheese

3 tablespoons maple syrup
or honey

Preheat the oven to 180°C. Lightly grease and flour a bundt tin.

Cream butter with poppy seeds until light and fluffy. Add honey and vanilla extract and beat well. Add eggs one at a time, beating well after each addition. Sift plain flour, bicarbonate of soda and salt into a bowl. Stir in sifted wholemeal flour. Fold dry ingredients into creamed mixture alternately with sour cream. Mix well.

Pour into prepared tin and bake for 50–60 minutes. Allow to cool.

To make topping, soften cream cheese and beat in maple syrup until smooth and creamy. Spread over cake.

Spicy Prune Cake

125 g butter

1 cup sugar

2 eggs

⅔ cup drained stewed stoned
   prunes (roughly chopped,
   reserve juice)

⅔ cup sour cream

1½ cups plain flour

½ teaspoon bicarbonate of soda

½ teaspoon salt

½ teaspoon ground nutmeg

½ teaspoon ground cinnamon

½ teaspoon allspice

ICING

1 tablespoon softened butter

2 cups icing sugar

½ teaspoon ground cinnamon

2 tablespoons reserved prune
   juice

Preheat the oven to 180°C. Lightly grease and flour two sandwich tins.

Cream butter and sugar. Add eggs one at a time, beating well, then prunes
and sour cream. Fold in sifted dry ingredients.

Pour into prepared tins and bake for 30–40 minutes. Turn out onto a rack
to cool.

To make icing, beat ingredients together, adding enough prune juice
to make a smooth, spreadable icing. Fill and ice cake when cold.

Strawberry Shortcake

1½ cups self-raising flour
½ teaspoon baking powder
good pinch of salt
75 g softened butter
½ cup castor sugar
1 egg, beaten
¼ cup buttermilk

FILLING

250 g strawberries, hulled,
    halved and mixed with
    1 dessertspoon castor sugar
200 ml cream, whipped

icing sugar, for dusting

Preheat the oven to 190°C. Lightly grease two 20-cm round cake tins and line the bases with non-stick baking paper.

Combine the sifted flour, baking powder and salt in a large mixing bowl. Add the butter and rub into the flour until the mixture resembles coarse breadcrumbs. Mix in the sugar and the egg. Stir in enough buttermilk to form a soft dough. Divide mixture into two and, with floured hands, press lightly into the tins.

Bake for 20–25 minutes or until firm and lightly browned. Turn out onto a rack to cool.

Fill with strawberries and whipped cream, and dust with icing sugar.

Streusel Pumpkin Cake

60 g softened butter

⅓ cup castor sugar

⅓ cup mashed pumpkin

¼ cup sour cream

1 egg, lightly beaten

1¼ cups plain flour

¼ teaspoon grated nutmeg

1 tablespoon baking powder

½ teaspoon bicarbonate of soda

⅓ cup orange juice

2 teaspoons grated orange zest

TOPPING

¼ cup brown sugar

45 g chilled butter, cut into small pieces

2 tablespoons plain flour

½ teaspoon ground cinnamon

⅓ cup pecans, roughly chopped

Preheat the oven to 180°C. Lightly grease a 22-cm round springform cake tin and line the base with non-stick baking paper.

Beat the butter, sugar, pumpkin, sour cream and egg until well combined.

Sift the flour, nutmeg, baking powder and bicarbonate of soda into another bowl. Make a well in the centre and stir in the pumpkin mixture and orange juice, alternating between the two, until well combined. Stir in the orange zest. ➤

Pour the batter into the prepared tin.

Combine the streusel topping ingredients in a bowl until the mixture resembles coarse breadcrumbs. Sprinkle the mixture over the cake batter.

Bake for 45 minutes or until firm and cooked through. Cool in the tin and then turn out onto a rack.

Serve warm or cold with cream or yoghurt.

Sultana Lunch Cake

350 g sultanas

225 g butter

1 cup sugar

3 eggs

3⅓ cups plain flour

3 teaspoons baking powder

½ teaspoon salt

½ cup milk

Preheat the oven to 180°C. Lightly grease a 20-cm cake tin and line the bottom with non-stick baking paper.

Cover sultanas with water and boil for 10 minutes. Strain and cool. Cream butter and sugar, then add eggs one at a time, beating well. Add sultanas, sifted flour, baking powder and salt. Stir in milk.

Pour into prepared tin and bake for 90 minutes, or until cooked.

Syd's Lamingtons

150 g softened butter

⅔ cup castor sugar

2 eggs

½ teaspoon vanilla extract

4 tablespoons milk

275 g self-raising flour

ICING

3 tablespoons cocoa

3 tablespoons drinking chocolate

3 tablespoons water

3 tablespoons castor sugar

30 g butter

2½ cups desiccated coconut, for decorating

Preheat the oven to 180°C. Lightly grease a 25-cm × 20-cm lamington pan and line with non-stick baking paper.

Cream the butter and sugar until light and fluffy. In another bowl, beat the eggs, vanilla extract and milk. Slowly beat this mixture into the butter mixture. Fold in the sifted flour and add more milk if necessary to form a smooth batter.

Pour into the prepared pan and bake for 30 minutes or until golden. Cool for 5 minutes before turning out onto a rack to cool completely. **>**

Meanwhile, stir all the icing ingredients in a saucepan over a gentle heat for 5–6 minutes, until the mixture is smooth and glossy. Remove and cool a little.

When the cake is completely cold, cut into twenty squares. Using tongs or piercing the cake with a metal skewer, dip each square into the icing to completely cover it, then roll in the coconut. Continue until all the cakes have been iced and covered with coconut.

Tamarillo Nut Cake

100 g butter
¾ cup sugar
2 eggs, beaten
¾ cup drained cooked
  tamarillos (see below)
1½ cups plain flour
½ teaspoon bicarbonate of soda
pinch of ground nutmeg
1 teaspoon ground cinnamon

¼ cup chopped walnuts
½ cup sultanas

ICING

1 cup icing sugar
1 tablespoon lemon juice
1–2 tablespoons water

walnuts, for decorating

Preheat the oven to 180°C. Lightly grease and flour an 18-cm ring tin.

In a large bowl cream butter and sugar. Add eggs and combine well. To cook tamarillos, peel, chop and stew gently until soft. Finely chop cooked tamarillos and add to creamed mixture alternately with sifted dry ingredients. Fold in chopped walnuts and sultanas.

Pour into prepared tin and bake for 75 minutes or until cooked.

Allow to cool in tin. Combine icing ingredients and drizzle over cake. Decorate top with walnuts.

Traditional Baked Cheesecake

BASE

50 g rolled oats

100 g sweet biscuit crumbs

75 g butter, melted

FILLING

3 eggs, separated

150 g castor sugar

300 g cream cheese

1 tablespoon plain flour

grated zest and juice of 1 lemon

50 g sultanas

100 ml sour cream

Preheat the oven to 170°C. Lightly grease a 20-cm springform cake tin and line the base with non-stick baking paper.

Combine the base ingredients and press into the base of the prepared tin. Refrigerate while you make the filling.

Whisk the egg yolks together with the sugar until thick and creamy. Beat in the cream cheese, sifted flour, zest and juice. Fold in the sultanas and the sour cream. Whip the egg whites until stiff and then carefully fold them through the egg-yolk mixture.

Pour into the prepared tin and bake for 60 minutes or until firm to the touch. Cool completely before serving with orange segments and chopped strawberries.

Treacle, Prune & Walnut Loaf

175 g self-raising flour

175 g wholemeal flour

½ teaspoon salt

½ teaspoon bicarbonate of soda

50 g walnuts, roughly chopped

75 g stoned prunes, roughly chopped

275 ml buttermilk

2 tablespoons treacle

Preheat the oven to 200°C. Lightly grease and line a 25-cm × 15-cm loaf pan with non-stick baking paper.

Sift the flours into a mixing bowl with the salt and bicarbonate of soda. Mix in the chopped walnuts and prunes.

Warm the buttermilk in a saucepan and stir in the treacle until it has dissolved. Make a well in the centre of the flour mixture and stir in the buttermilk mixture. Fold quickly to make a soft dough.

Pour into the prepared pan and bake for 30–35 minutes or until firm and cooked through. Cool in the tin and then turn out onto a rack.

This loaf is delicious served with cheddar cheese or a salty blue cheese.

Tropical Fruit Salad Cake

3 cups plain flour

1 teaspoon salt

1 teaspoon bicarbonate of soda

1 teaspoon garam masala or
   ground cinnamon

2 cups sugar

3 eggs, beaten

1½ cups safflower or corn oil

1½ teaspoons vanilla extract

1 × 250-g tin crushed pineapple,
   undrained

2 cups chopped very ripe
   bananas

FILLING

50 g butter

250 g cream cheese

1 teaspoon vanilla extract

1½ cups icing sugar

pawpaw or mango for filling

Preheat the oven to 180°C. Lightly grease and flour three 18-cm sponge tins.

Sift dry ingredients into large bowl with sugar. Add eggs and oil, stirring well. Do not beat. Stir in vanilla extract, pineapple and banana.

Spoon the batter into the three prepared tins and bake for 25–30 minutes, or until cooked. Allow to cool in tins for 10 minutes before removing.

To make cream cheese filling, beat together all ingredients. Spread filling on top of all three cakes. Layer the cakes, spreading small pieces of pawpaw or mango on top of the filling between layers.

Turkish Fig & Chocolate Cake

¾ cup chopped dried figs

½ cup brandy

120 g butter

⅔ cup castor sugar

3 eggs

1½ cups roasted hazelnuts, chopped finely

125 g dark cooking chocolate, chopped

¼ cup dried breadcrumbs

ICING

⅓ cup sugar

100 g milk chocolate, chopped

½ cup cream

Preheat the oven to 160°C. Lightly grease a 23-cm springform tin and line the base with non-stick baking paper.

Combine figs and brandy in a saucepan and boil until brandy has evaporated. Allow to cool.

Cream butter and sugar, add eggs and beat well. Add figs and brandy (don't worry if this mixture looks curdled). Melt chocolate in a bowl over hot water. Stir nuts, melted chocolate and breadcrumbs into fig mixture.

Pour into prepared tin and bake for 60–75 minutes. Allow to cool on a rack.

To make icing, heat sugar in saucepan until brown. Add chocolate and heat gently until melted – don't boil. Remove from heat, add cream and mix well. Allow mixture to cool to room temperature before icing – it will thicken as it cools.

Upside-down Caramel Banana Pudding

60 g butter

¼ cup brown sugar

3 large ripe bananas, thinly
  sliced

40 g walnut halves

250 g softened butter

1½ cups brown sugar

1⅓ cups self-raising flour

2 level teaspoons baking powder

50 g chopped walnuts

3 tablespoons milk

Preheat the oven to 180°C. Lightly grease a 2-litre shallow ovenproof dish or cake tin.

Melt the butter and sugar in a saucepan over a low heat. Spread over the base and sides of the prepared dish and lay the banana slices over the top. Place the walnut halves into any gaps.

Blend the remaining ingredients together in a food processor or using an electric mixer.

Spread the mixture over the bananas and bake for 50 minutes or until the pudding is cooked through and golden brown on top. Run a knife around the edges and turn out onto a hot dish.

Serve warm or cold.

SERVES 6

Vintage Victoria Sponge Cake with Cream & Jam

225 g softened butter

1 cup castor sugar

4 eggs

1½ cups self-raising flour

2 teaspoons baking powder

¼ cup strawberry or raspberry jam

150 ml cream, whipped

icing sugar, for dusting

Preheat the oven to 180°C. Lightly grease two 20-cm sandwich cake tins and line the bases with non-stick baking paper.

Combine the butter, sugar, eggs, sifted flour and baking powder and beat until well blended and thoroughly mixed to a creamy batter. Divide the mixture between the two cake tins.

Bake for 25–30 minutes or until lightly browned and cooked through.

Cool in the tin for 10 minutes. Turn out onto a rack to cool completely.

Fill with jam and cream and dust with icing sugar.

Walnut Fudge Cake

¾ cup brown sugar

150 g butter

100 g dark cooking chocolate,
    chopped

½ cup condensed milk

2 cups chopped walnuts

¾ cup self-raising flour

¼ cup milk

1 egg, lightly beaten

icing sugar, for dusting

Preheat the oven to 180°C. Lightly grease a 20-cm round cake tin and line the base with non-stick baking paper.

Heat the sugar, butter, chocolate, condensed milk and walnuts in a saucepan, stirring over a low heat until the mixture has thickened and the sugar is dissolved.

Remove from the heat and cool a little. Pour into a mixing bowl. Stir in the sifted flour, milk and egg until well combined. Spoon into the prepared tin and smooth the top.

Bake for 30–40 minutes or until cooked through but still moist in the middle. Cool in the tin before cutting and dusting with icing sugar.

Serve with ice-cream.

Walnut Victoria Sandwich

175 g butter

175 g castor sugar

3 eggs, beaten

175 g self-raising flour

pinch of salt

2 tablespoons warm water

jam, for filling

walnuts, for decorating

Preheat the oven to 190°C. Lightly grease two 18-cm sandwich tins and line the bases with non-stick baking paper.

Cream butter and sugar until light and fluffy. Beat in eggs. Sift flour and salt. Stir 1 tablespoon of flour into butter mixture until well mixed. Gradually beat in remaining flour. Add enough water to give a soft dropping consistency.

Pour into prepared tins and bake for 20 minutes, or until well risen and golden. Turn out onto a rack to cool.

Fill with jam. Ice with Glacé Icing (see page 214) and decorate with walnuts.

Warm Upside-down Ricotta Cakes with Melba Sauce

BASE

1 cup sweet biscuit crumbs

3 tablespoons softened butter

FILLING

¼ cup cream cheese

1 cup ricotta cheese

½ teaspoon vanilla extract

½ teaspoon almond extract

2 large eggs, lightly beaten

3 tablespoons castor sugar

SAUCE

300 g tinned or frozen
   raspberries

2 tablespoons redcurrant jelly

½ tablespoon icing sugar

1 tablespoon arrowroot, mixed
   with 1 tablespoon cold water

Preheat the oven to 180°C. Lightly grease a six-cup jumbo muffin tin.

Combine the biscuit crumbs and butter and press into the bases of
the muffin cups.

Beat the filling ingredients until smooth. Spoon evenly into the muffin cups.
Bake for 15–20 minutes or until set. Cool for 10 minutes before turning out.

To make Melba sauce, rub the raspberries through a sieve to remove
all the seeds. Place in a saucepan and add the redcurrant jelly and icing
sugar. Slowly bring to the boil and then turn the heat down and stir in the
arrowroot. Continue stirring until the sauce has thickened (2–3 minutes).

Serve cakes upside down, drizzled with Melba sauce.

Whisked Sponge Cake with Coffee Icing

3 large eggs

125 g castor sugar

85 g self-raising flour

ICING

2 cups icing sugar

200 g softened butter

2 teaspoons instant coffee dissolved in 2 tablespoons boiling water

½ cup chocolate-coated coffee beans, for decorating

Preheat the oven to 190°C. Lightly grease a 20-cm round cake tin and line the base with non-stick baking paper.

Beat the eggs and sugar until pale and thick. Sift the flour into the mixture and carefully fold through.

Pour into the cake tin and bake for 30–35 minutes or until firm and cooked through.

Turn out onto a rack to cool. When cold, cut in half horizontally.

To make icing, place icing sugar in a food processor and pulse to remove any lumps. Add butter and coffee and process until smooth. Carefully, using a spatula, spread about one-third of the icing as a filling for the cake. Spread the rest of the icing to cover the whole cake. Decorate with chocolate-coated coffee beans around the top and sides.

Wicked Marbled Chocolate Pudding

50 g dark cooking chocolate, chopped

50 g white chocolate, chopped

110 g softened butter

⅔ cup brown sugar

2 eggs, beaten

¾ cup self-raising flour

SAUCE

100 g dark cooking chocolate, chopped

150 ml cream

Preheat the oven to 190°C, or fill a steaming pan with water. Lightly grease a 900-ml pudding basin.

Melt the chocolates separately in bowls over hot water.

Cream the butter and sugar until light and fluffy. Add the eggs, a little at a time and then fold in the sifted flour. Spoon half of the mixture into another bowl and stir in the melted dark chocolate. Stir the white chocolate into the other half of the mixture. Spoon the white and dark chocolate mixtures into the prepared basin alternately. Using a wooden skewer, swirl through the mixture to create a marbled effect.

Cover with greased, pleated foil. Bake for 90 minutes, or steam for 90 minutes on top of the stove, topping up with water as necessary.

To make hot chocolate sauce, place ingredients in a saucepan over a gentle heat and stir until the sauce is smooth and glossy.

SERVES 6

Zucchini Cake

500 g grated zucchini

1 cup vegetable oil

1½ cups brown sugar

2½ cups plain flour

1½ teaspoons baking powder

1½ teaspoons ground cinnamon

1 teaspoon grated nutmeg

½ teaspoon salt

3 eggs, beaten

1 cup chopped walnuts

½ cup sultanas

icing sugar, for dusting

Preheat the oven to 160°C. Lightly grease and flour a 23-cm round tin.

Combine zucchini, oil and sugar. Allow to stand for 5 minutes. Add sifted dry ingredients, eggs, walnuts and sultanas.

Pour into prepared tin and bake for 90 minutes, or until cooked.

Dust with icing sugar or ice as required.

Icings & Sauces

Butterscotch Sauce

¾ cup castor sugar

¼ cup boiling water

¾ cup brown sugar

50 g butter

few drops vanilla extract

100 ml cream

Dissolve the castor sugar in a saucepan over a gentle heat and bring to the boil. Cook until the syrup turns a golden brown.

Off the heat, pour in the boiling water and stir. Stir in the brown sugar and butter and return to the heat until the mixture is smooth and the sugar is dissolved. Stir in the vanilla and cream and cool until ready to serve.

Chocolate Icing

150 g icing sugar

2 tablespoons cocoa

1 teaspoon softened or melted butter

1–2 tablespoons warm water

Sift icing sugar and cocoa. Add melted butter to warm water, then gradually mix into sugar until a smooth paste is formed.

Cream Cheese Icing

250 g softened cream cheese

50 g softened butter

1 teaspoon vanilla extract

500 g icing sugar

Using a food processor or electric mixer, blend the cream cheese and butter. Add the vanilla extract, then mix in the sifted icing sugar until smooth. Refrigerate until ready to use.

Glacé Icing

150 g icing sugar

1 teaspoon softened or melted butter

1–2 tablespoons warm water

Sift icing sugar. Add butter to warm water, then gradually mix into sugar until a smooth paste is formed.

Lemon Icing

2 cups icing sugar

1 teaspoon softened butter

2 tablespoons lemon juice

Sift icing sugar. Beat together icing sugar, butter and enough lemon juice to give a spreading consistency.

Orange Icing

225 g softened butter

225 g icing sugar

grated zest and juice of
  ½ an orange

In a food processor or electric
mixer, cream the butter and icing
sugar until light and fluffy. Slowly
mix in the orange zest and juice
until smooth.

Pouring Custard

2 eggs

1 tablespoon castor sugar

1 cup milk

few drops vanilla extract

Using a whisk, mix the eggs and
sugar lightly. Heat the milk and
vanilla extract in a saucepan until
just warmed through. Remove
from heat and pour over the eggs.

Tip the mixture back into the
saucepan and, stirring all the time,
slowly bring to the boil. Turn down
immediately to a simmer and cook,
still stirring constantly, until the
custard is thick enough to coat
the back of a spoon.

Serve hot or cold.

To serve cold, whisk custard in
a stainless steel bowl over a bowl
of ice until cool, to avoid splitting.

Index

PENGUIN BOOKS

Published by the Penguin Group
Penguin Group (Australia)
250 Camberwell Road, Camberwell, Victoria 3124, Australia
(a division of Pearson Australia Group Pty Ltd)
Penguin Group (USA) Inc.
375 Hudson Street, New York, New York 10014, USA
Penguin Group (Canada)
90 Eglinton Avenue East, Suite 700, Toronto ON M4P 2Y3, Canada
(a division of Pearson Penguin Canada Inc.)
Penguin Books Ltd
80 Strand, London WC2R 0RL, England
Penguin Ireland
25 St Stephen's Green, Dublin 2, Ireland
(a division of Penguin Books Ltd)
Penguin Books India Pvt Ltd
11 Community Centre, Panchsheel Park, New Delhi – 110 017, India
Penguin Group (NZ)
Cnr Airborne and Rosedale Roads, Albany, Auckland, New Zealand
(a division of Pearson New Zealand Ltd)
Penguin Books (South Africa) (Pty) Ltd
24 Sturdee Avenue, Rosebank, Johannesburg 2196, South Africa

Penguin Books Ltd, Registered Offices: 80 Strand, London, WC2R 0RL, England

First published by Penguin Group (Australia), 2006

10 9 8 7 6 5 4 3 2 1

Many thanks go to photographer Julie Renouf, baker Kerryn Vilinskis, and Dora Nitsopoulos of Paper
Occasions in Ivanhoe, Victoria, who provided a selection of the beautiful props.

Design by Elizabeth Theodosiadis © Penguin Group (Australia)
Cover photograph by Julie Renouf
Typeset by Post Pre-press Group, Brisbane, Queensland
Printed in China by Everbest Printing Co. Ltd

National Library of Australia
Cataloguing-in-Publication data:

Cake Bible.
Includes index.
ISBN-13: 978 0 14 300520 9
ISBN-10: 0 14 300520 0
1. Cake.

641.8653

www.penguin.com.au